Architecture in Perspective

Architecture in Perspective

A five year Retrospective of Award Winning Illustration

The American Society of Architectural Perspectivists

VNR VAN NOSTRAND REINHOLD
New York

Acknowledgments

The American Society of Architectural Perspectivists must extend a collective word of thanks to the many groups and individuals who have helped make this book a reality:

To the editorial and production staffs of Van Nostrand Reinhold Company for their professionalism and skill. And especially to Ms. Wendy Lochner for her support, loyalty, and belief in ASAP.

To Mr. Paul Stevenson Oles, FAIA, co-founder of ASAP, for the Society's historical underpinnings recounted in his foreword.

To Mr. Frank Costantino, co-founder of ASAP, and Mr. Thomas W. Schaller, AIA, President Emeritus, for their extensive contributions to the text and production coordination.

To Eliza Beckwith, Catherine Costantino, Elizabeth Day, Kirk Doggett, William Hook and Cynthia O'Connell for their tireless efforts in the compilation of material and production assistance. To the executive administrator of ASAP, Mrs. Janis Connor for always being there and helping us keep things "in perspective."

To the indefatigable Mr. John Deputy for his graphic talents and extraordinary efforts in book design and production.

To the fifteen jurors, distinguished professionals all, without whose valuable time, depth of experience, and acuity of judgement, this collection of noteworthy drawings would not be possible.

To the many regional chapters, and the national office of the American Institute of Architects, whose enthusiasm for perspective drawing has garnered their staunch support; and the many other venues that hosted our exhibitions and provided the public forum for our work.

And finally to the membership—the many gifted men and women whose talents may or may not be displayed herein, but whose passion for perspectivism and generosity in their support of the profession, and especially for the survival of ASAP, have helped raise the standards of architectural artwork to a measurable, and enduring, degree.

Copyright © 1992 by Van Nostrand Reinhold

Library of Congress Catalog Card Number 91-28736
ISBN 0-442-00700-0

Printed in Hong Kong by Excel Printing Company

Designed by John Deputy.

Van Nostrand Reinhold
115 Fifth Avenue
New York, NY 10003

Chapman and Hall
2-6 Boundary Row
London, SE1 8HN, England

Thomas Nelson Australia
102 Dodds Street
South Melbourne 3205
Victoria, Australia

Nelson Canada
1120 Birchmount Road
Scarborough, Ontario M1K 5G4, Canada

16 15 14 13 12 11 10 9 8 7 6 5 4 3 2 1

Library of Congress Cataloging-in- Publication Data

Architecture in perspective : a five year retrospective of award
-winning illustrations / American Society of Architectural
Perspectivists.
    p. cm.
    Includes index.
    ISBN 0-442-00700-0
    1. Architectural rendering--United States--Awards Exhibitions.
I. American Society of Architectural Perspectivists.
NA2780.A73   1991
720'.22'27309043--dc20   91-28736
                                                                  CIP

Contents

Foreword   vi

Preface   viii

Architecture in Perspective I   9

Architecture in Perspective II   43

Architecture in Perspective III   81

Architecture in Perspective IV   113

Architecture in Perspective V   157

Artists' Directory and Commentary   198

Foreword

On one of July's hottest days, three Boston perspectivists sat at lunch around a small cafe table discussing the question of why architectural artists rarely talk with each other. Steve Rich, Frank Costantino and Steve Oles found no satisfactory answer, other than the lack of a structured means to encourage such dialogue. Perhaps by organizing a modest exhibition of architectural drawings they might provide a point of contact for local architects and artists who had drawn quietly and alone for years.

So, on September 20, 1984, the "First Annual Architectural Delineators Exhibition" emerged for a total of four hours in the lounge of the Boston Architectural Center. Despite the brief nature of the show, it generated an amazingly positive response among participants and viewers. It was unanimously agreed there would be a second annual exhibition.

In the autumn of that following year, the invited exhibition was held for four weeks in the BAC's main gallery. Sixty-eight works by thirty-three artists, from Maine to Pennsylvania, were displayed with a special group of eight Australian pieces. Robert Campbell, architecture critic for *The Boston Globe*, praised the show in a review titled "Revival of Fine Drawing Gains Momentum."

With the momentum of this success and to the question of "what next?," the response seemed obvious—to "go national." In March, 1986, branded with a new logo and an official address at the BAC, the American Society of Architectural Perspectivists was brought into being. In October of 1986, the inaugural juried exhibition/competition was the first truly national representation of work, selected by a jury of three respected professionals from the fields of architecture, education and illustration. This interdisciplinary composition has remained ASAP's principal guideline for selection of jurors.

Through its first five years, ASAP has benefitted from the judgments of fifteen excellent jurors including seven Fellows of the American Institute of Architects, four internationally known perspectivists, six multi-skilled and highly accomplished architect/artist/educators, and two eminent professionals from the curatorial and publishing fields. Because the annual exhibition and its attendant catalogue are the most visible and consequential events sponsored by the Society, the careful selection of each year's jury is therefore regarded as a matter of utmost importance.

Since that initial four-hour display, there have been three subsequent shows in Boston and more than two dozen exhibition venues of varying duration all across the United States and Canada. New York, Washington, D.C., California, Illinois, Michigan, Nevada, and Texas have hosted at least two exhibitions each while Florida, Minnesota, Oregon, and Missouri have provided single venues. Architecture In Perspective has appeared at every national AIA convention since 1987.

These exhibitions have been duly noted with generous coverage by the professional press in this country, Japan, England, and China. Reviews have appeared in *The Chicago Tribune, The Dallas Morning News, The New York Times, The Boston Globe*, as well as the major architectural journals.

While the membership has presently stabilized between three and four hundred (including approximately one hundred Canadian members), as many as a thousand perspectivists have at some time been members of the Society. Many members seek and enjoy frequent contact with their colleagues in England (through the Society of Architectural and Industrial Illustrators) and Japan (with the Japanese Architectural Renderers Association). ASAP started with one international coordinator (Japan) and now boasts seven. Similarly, the three original domestic advisory councillors have increased to fifteen.

The early policies and procedures of the Society were determined and personally directed almost solely by its three founders, but a more demo-cratic —and structured—organization, governed by elected officers and formal by-laws, were later developed. ASAP has obtained tax-exempt corporate status, with a paid (and constantly harried) executive administrator.

A key tenet of all officers is that "inclusivism" should be a guiding principal of the Society. To that end, membership has remained open to all, fees have been kept reasonable, and ecuminism has been encouraged. The election of our first Canadian president in 1992 will be a welcome step toward a more cosmopolitan and inclusive Society.

As this organization confidently matures, it is appropriate to acknowledge as instrumental to the successes, the reviews, and the impressive numbers which now define the Society, its early advocates and supporters. In addition to the substantial personal funds contributed by the founders to underwrite the printing costs of the first catalogue, the publishing company of Van Nostrand Reinhold deserves recognition for its generous, sustained support. The Boston Architectural Center and its director, Bernard Spring, FAIA, provided a home, without which ASAP could not have flourished. Boston architect and charter member, A. Anthony Tappé, FAIA, has been a trusted advisor from the very beginning. Also to be remembered are the timely monetary gifts of the late Suda Willis Oles. Without the help of these and many other self-less, dedicated, and energetic people, ASAP would today remain only the acronym for "as soon as possible."

Paul Stevenson Oles, FAIA
Boston, Massachusetts

FOUNDERS
Oles, Rich, Costantino (facing page)

Preface

Drawing, it has been said, is the language of architecture. Surely one of the most abiding images of an architect is that of the lone individual, pencil in hand, giving face and form to our homes, our offices, our cities. Notwithstanding the innumerable changes that time and technology, politics and economics have wrought upon the design professions, this image was, and to some extent continues to be, true. Though more often than not, the "lone individual" is a member of a design team, many final construction drawings are now computer-generated. However, there is still no adequate substitute in the architectural design professions for men and women who can draw—who can communicate—with a pencil, a pen, or a brush.

The professsion of perspectivist—a specialist who graphically represents proposed architectural design—has come to light only within the past one hundred years. While the basic tenets of accurate perspective construction have been common knowledge to painters and draughtsmen since the Rennaissance, the application of these tenets to the practice of architectural design has been less long-lived. From their roots in France in the 1700s, the teachings and techniques of the Ecole-des-Beaux-Arts have had long-standing, pervasive, and persuasive influences upon design and drawing throughout Europe and America until the present day. Faithfully followed, the rigorous Beaux-Arts discipline and classical principles permitted the graphic representation of architecture in orthogonal drawings only, i.e.: plan, section, and elevation. It took the influence of architectural theorists, such as Piranesi and especially the British topographical painters to make perspective drawings an accepted element of architectural design practice by the 19th century. Near the end of the 19th century and through the early to mid-20th, as architects themselves became more occupied with the completion of actual construction documents,

they became accustomed to securing the services of free-lance perspectivists—architects and artists who had greater skill with pen, pencil, or brush than the designing architect.

The past several years have been witness to nothing short of a renaissance of architectural artwork. As architectural tastes began to evolve rapidly in the late 1970s, remarkable examples of the perspectivist's art, in all mediums and from all levels of practice, began to emerge. Clearly, the profession was thriving and seemed to be one deserving of a voice, a forum. It was in this milieu and toward this end that ASAP was formed. Rather than merely capitalizing upon a trend, ASAP, more than any other single body, has been responsible for the general focussing of attention upon the diverse talents and unique skills which characterize the professional architectural artist. The primary activity to effect this attention has been ASAP's sponsorship of an open juried competition of architectural artwork—*Architecture in Perspective*. Since 1985, the competition has grown from an essentially local exhibit to have become in 1990, North America's (and arguably the world's) single most prestigious forum for architectural illustration.

This book highlights the talents of the artists represented herein—North America's most outstanding practitioners of the perspectivist's art—and showcases the selected pieces from ASAP's first five competitions. Moreover, by presenting these drawings in chronological format, this retrospective may serve not only as a barometer of the profession of architectural design and drawing from the mid-1980s onward, but will also afford the reader a better understanding of the evolution of a unique field of endeavor. These are the men and women who with pen, pencil, or paintbrush give face and form, life and spirit, to our as-yet unbuilt environment. They are truly the voice of architecture.

Architecture In Perspective

I

Introduction

Steve Oles

Architecture in Perspective I, held at The Boston Architectural Center in 1986, was the first exhibition of architectural delineation to be sponsored and displayed under the auspices of the newly formed American Society of Architectural Perspectivists. It was also the first to be structured as a drawing competition and juried by a small panel of distinguished design professionals—three seeming to be the optimum number. As in subsequent years, the jury selection was intended to garner the objective opinions of various disciplines related to the field of perspectivism; specifically, the worlds of design, academia, the arts, and professional delineation itself. And while the names, faces, and places would change from year to year, this was to become the format for all Architecture in Perspective competitions.

Jurors for the first official Architecture in Perspective exhibition, which was displayed at the Boston Architectural Center from 6 October to 14 November 1986, were Arizona State University Professor William Kirby Lockard FAIA; Boston architect A. Anthony Tappé, FAIA; and architectural delineator Brian Burr. Their straightforward and somewhat unrestrictive charge was to select approximately sixty works, as varied in style, technique, and approach as possible, for exhibition—no small task in light of the four hundred sixty-seven submittals received from artists in twenty-eight states across the nation.

As in all following competitions, the entrants' work was judged in slide format only, ensuring as much consistency and fairness as possible in the comparison process. Initially, slides were viewed on light tables until a group of one hundred fifty was chosen for projection during the final jury process. In later competitions, all slides were projected from the initial rounds to the final selections. It is important to note that of the sixty-some works selected for display from forty-one different artists, only one image per artist was printed in the accompanying exhibit catalogue, *Architecture in Perspective*. The release of this book marks the first printing for some previously unpublished selections, in addition to the works from all Architecture In Perspective exhibitions.

In assessing their precedent-setting role, juror Lockard wrote; "Because this was the very first ASAP competition, Anthony Tappé, Brian Burr, and I were concerned with establishing a very broad range of rendering techniques, as well as subject matter, so that those perspectives selected would not seem to limit the diversity of perspectivists who might belong to the newly founded Society. We didn't have to look far into the entries to be assured that there was plenty of diversity…a diversity in medium, in technique, and in subject matter that was really remarkable."

Aside from the request of ASAP's executive board that the jurors select the highest quality and varied a group of works as possible, there were few guidelines for the inclusion of work in Architecture in Perspective. Lockard continued, "…we decided not to limit the entries of this first exhibition only to perspectives, accepting, after some discussion, Shu Xiang Xi's beautifully rendered section. It was also interesting to see that several of the very best drawings, including one of the 'Best of Show' drawings by Lee Dunnette, followed the tradition of including other architectural drawings in an overall composition." As would prove to be the case with successive jurors, the qualitative effect of the architectural design on the quality of the final artwork was decidedly an

issue. But as Lockard asserted, "…in looking back over five years of exhibitions, I believe we need not have worried too much, because the drawings allow some very interesting buildings, standing as testaments to the perspectivist's own design skill or a very commendable discretion in what they chose to draw."

The jury agreed that the title "Best of Show" be reserved for as many as three examples of work which they considered deserving of this honor. In 1986, two such awards were given: to architect/illustrator Lee Dunnette of New York for his remarkably executed mixed-media composition, "Worth Square Building;" and to illustrator James Record of Fort Worth, Texas, for an astounding pencil rendition of the Texas Statehouse cupola. These works, and the others selected for the inaugural exhibition, may be seen on the following pages. It is in fact Mr. Dunnette's piece, as the very first "Best in Show" of the Architecture in Perspective competitions, which graces the cover of this volume.

ARCHITECTURE IN PERSPECTIVE I 1986
Jurors Lockard, Tappé, and Burr (facing page)

Book Notes
A project title marked with an asterisk is a Category "B" entry.
The project architect follows the title.
Dimensions indicate height x width (inches).

Best of Show

Sharing "Best of Show" honors for the premier Architecture in Perspective exhibition was an example of remarkable pencil work by artist/ illustrator James Record. The term "pencil drawing" barely begins to describe the efforts of the Fort Worth native. Record had relocated to California when he received the commission to execute a drawing of the restoration of the Texas State Capitol dome in Austin, and had to return home to Texas to begin work on what was to be a true tour de force.

Although Mr. Record's piece was in effect a topographical drawing (the depiction of an existing structure), the quality and virtuosity of its execution most highly impressed the jury of Architecture in Perspective I. In following years, competition guidelines would permit the submission of drawings of "time-removed" projects only (those not wholly extant at the time of the drawing's completion).

The task of depicting the newly restored dome structure was far more demanding than the simple replication of a single photographic reference, since the size of the final work necessitated the painstaking construction of an accurate perspective base and the equally meticulous application of explicit detail in fine pencil line. Record had to use hundreds of small photographic detail shots for reference—incorporating them into the proper viewpoint. Without question, Record feels that this was the single most difficult drawing he has ever done. "The optical problems were phenomenal," he stated, having methodically completed the work from the top of the statue at the dome's apex on down. "Until that piece was absolutely finished I did not know if it was correct or not."

Eight months and over five hundred hours of labor were required to complete the drawing, which ultimately represents a view of the structure Record prizes as unique; "The only way this piece could be done is if an artist did what I did. You can't photograph this." The drawing, reproduced as a special edition commemorative print, became a well-recognized symbol for Texas' statehood sesquicentennial in 1986. Not only do prints hang in its executive offices, but copies are still effective for ongoing fund-raising for the extensive renovation of the Capitol.

Besides serving as a grand, historical document of the Capitol, befitting the largesse of the Lone Star state, Mr. Record's unique work will be a hallmark of unparalleled architectural draughtsmanship for years to come.

JAMES RECORD
The State Capitol Dome, Texas (facing page)
Texas Sesquicentennial Commission
Pencil on illustration board 27x21

Best of Show

"Worth Square" by New York architect/illustrator Lee Dunnette was also awarded the title "Best of Show" from Architecture in Perspective I. The wonderfully evocative mixed media work depicts a high-rise structure of the artist's own design, of a larger presentation proposing revisions to New York City's zoning laws (which recall the "City Beautiful" movement and planning ideals of Camillo Citte).

The work is a highly successful synthesis of the objective (implied architectural specificity) and the subjective (an evocation of mood supplied by dramatic use of color, lighting effects, and composition). An effective, although updated, use of the traditional Beaux-Arts technique of depicting a proposal with multiple images upon a single field conveyed both additional design data and added artistic texture. "The ideal, for me as an architect," wrote Mr. Dunnette, "is to fuse the rational and romantic realities of a building. Both aspects must be studied to create a complete design, and both realities should be depicted if one wishes to convey the complexity of any architectural conception." The dominance of the emotive perspective view over the more purely informational orthogonals also helps set a reponsive tone in the viewer. "Reality," mused Mr. Dunnette, "is always more varied and subtle than I can imagine. Placing a building in its context often forces a more creative approach, and studying the 'atmosphere' of the site (especially color over time) has often blown away a preconception of style. 'Worth Square,' both the building and the rendering, are classical, symmetrical designs. Perhaps as a reaction to the chaos of New York City, the chaos of two kids at home, or perhaps

penance for a misspent youth, I prefer formally ordered compositions."

Not one to insist on a purist's approach to media, Mr. Dunnette explained his mixed approach: "Worth Square" is a perfect example of my career as a (material) polygamist: I will use 'whatever gets me through the night.' If tap-dancing on the drawing would have the desired effect, I would dance."

And in a truly cosmoplitan spirit, he has observed: "New York is filled with amazing combinations of natural and manmade light (it's all done with mirrors). You need only to see the New York Life building on a rainy night to know that architecture is more than stone and steel." Whether his inspiration is drawn from tap-dancing through rainy nights on New York's streets or from the expedient excitement of unlikely media combinations, clearly Mr. Dunnette's expressive talents and visionary abilties let us know that his art is more than paper and paint.

LEE DUNNETTE, AIA
Worth Square Building, New York (facing page)
Lee Dunnette, AIA, Architect
Airbrush, watercolor, pencil 40x30

WORTH SQUARE
BUILDING

Selected Entries

RICHARD B. FERRIER, AIA
Bevoni Residence (right)
Richard B. Ferrier, AIA, Architect
Watercolor and pencil 23x30

ROLANDO LLANES
Courtyard Study (below)
Pencil and watercolor 22x30

MONGKOL TANSANTISUK
American Fletcher Building, Indianapolis (facing page)
The Stubbins Associates, Architects
Prismacolor on photo paper 16x11

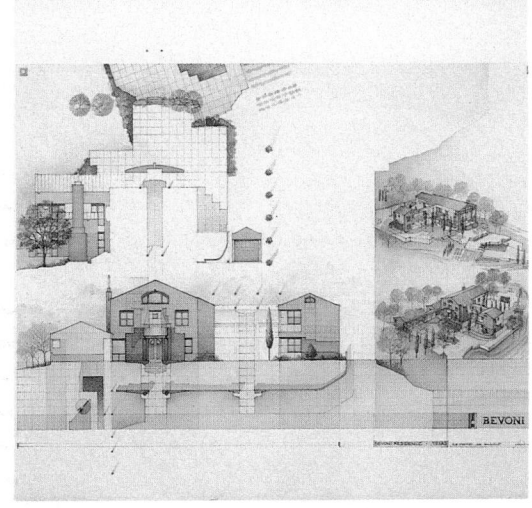

GENE STREET
River Cottages, Chicago (above)
Harry Weese, FAIA, Architect
Ink and marker 20x30

WENDY E. EVANS, AIA
Architectural Fantasy (left)
Wendy E. Evans, AIA, Architect
Watercolor 9x9

RICHARD C. BAEHR, AIA
International Place, Boston (facing page)
John Burgee, Philip Johnson, Architects
Tempera 35x23

OLD SOUTH CHURCH SANCTUARY ~ 1985

ROBERT W. COOK
Cliff House (facing page)
Prelim, Architects
Gouche 32x17

SHU-XIANG XI
Old South Church, Boston (above)
Shepley, Bulfinch, Richardson & Abbott, Architects
Watercolor 20x30

RANDY M. SOVICH, AIA
Henderson's Wharf, Baltimore (right)
RTKL Associates, Architects
Ink on white trace 11x14

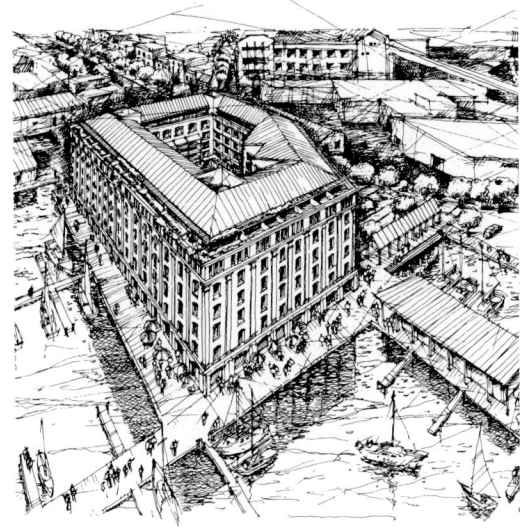

RICHARD C. MEYER
Grace Church, Darlington, Maryland (above)
Richard C. Meyer, Architect
Pencil on illustration board 12x21

DON M. JONES, AIA
Bryn Mawr Campus Center (left)
Bower Lewis Thrower, Architects
Color overlay on photograph 24x36

THOMAS W. SCHALLER
"Ideal" English House
Thomas Schaller, Architect
Watercolor 18x16

ANDY ANDERSON
One Kansas City Place
PBNI, Architects
Gouche and acrylic 35x30

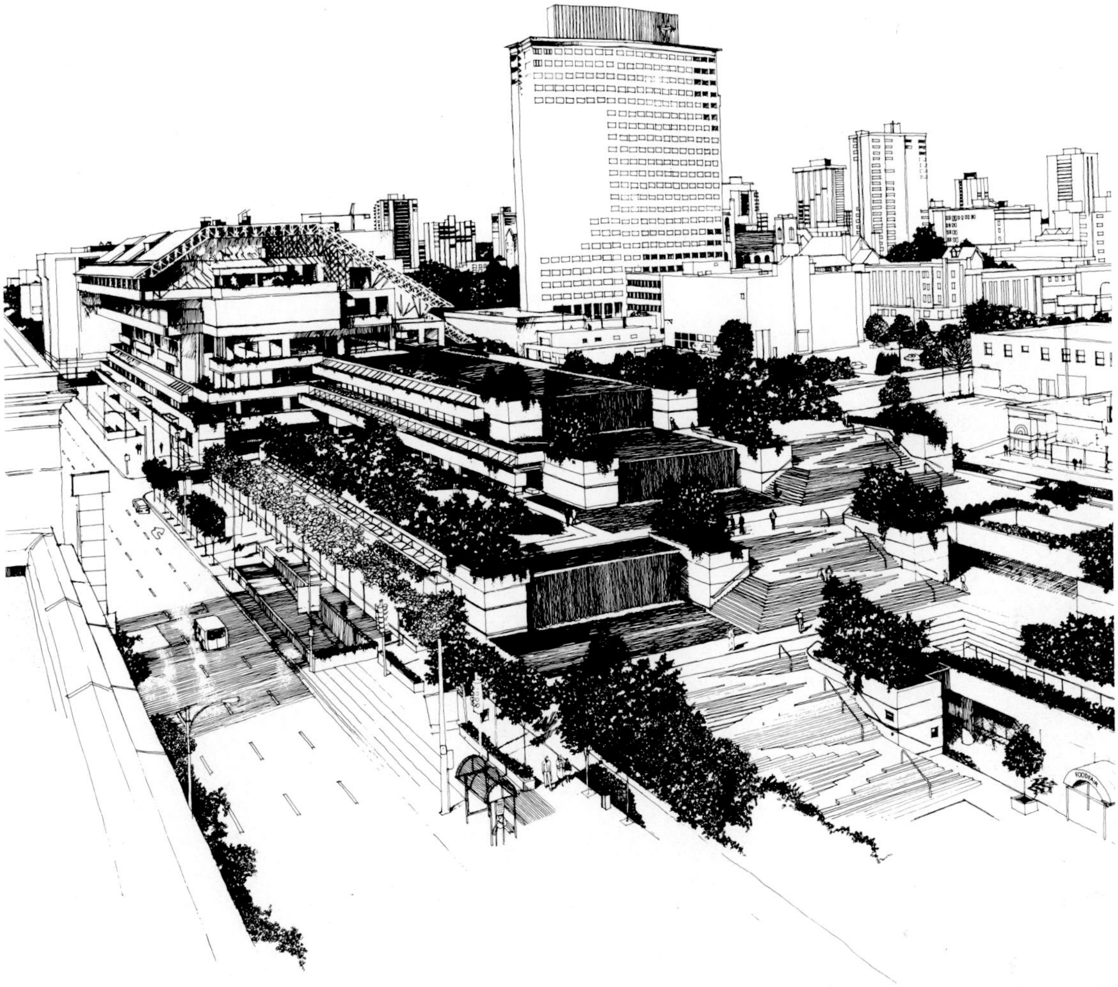

STEFAN A. TRENDOV
Vancouver City Complex (above)
Ink on mylar 42x30

ROBERT J. BERRY
Holiday Inn, Milford, MA (right)
Main Street Architects
Ink on mylar 20x24

HOUSE near QUISSETT HARBOUR · FALMOUTH, MASS.

PETER ADRIAN THOMAS
House near Quissett Harbor (facing page)
Lincoln Architects
Watercolor and ink 30x22

BON-HUI UY
Plaza view (above)
Pencil on mylar 23x26

BRUCE A. LAVALEE
Halcyon Limited, Architects (right)
Marker and gouche 24x30

PAUL SUN, FAIA
Union College, Schenectady, New York (left)
Shepley, Bulfinch, Richardson & Abbott, Architects
Ink and prismacolor 30x20

ROBIN SEN
CTS Chapel, Indianapolis (below)
Edward L. Barnes, FAIA, Architect
Prismacolor on illustration board 20x30

OREST ASSOCIATES
Intercontinental Hotel Competition (facing page)
Architecture Orest, Architects
Tempera 30x20

COMPLETION COMPETITION
HOTEL INTERCONTINENTAL

ARCHITECTURE OREST

JAMES EARL
Riverbend Office Park, Watertown, MA
Swain Associates, Architects
Pen, marker, pencil 18x13

AKIRA SATO, AIA
Adams Residence (above)
The BJSS Group, Architects
Pen, marker, pencil 18x12

STEPHAN S. EVANUSA, AIA
Syrigos Residence (right)
Hugh Newell Jacobsen, FAIA, Architect
Ink on mylar 30x20

JEFFREY M. GEORGE
101 Federal Street, Boston
Kohn Pedersen Fox, Architects
Colored pencil 18x16

SUNDAY MORNING AT QUINCY GATE

REMMERT W. HUYGENS, FAIA
Longy School of Music, Cambridge, MA (above)
Huygens & DiMella, Architects
Pencil 30x40

FREDERIC SCHWARTZ, AIA
Quincy Gate, Harvard University (right)
Frederic Schwartz, AIA, Architect
Collage 16x20

HENRY SORENSON
Big Sky Condominium, Montana (left)
Pencil 16x20

SUSAN AUSTIN-SALVO
Lake Center Executive Park (below)
F. Daniel Cathers & Associates, Architects
Pen and ink, prismacolor 30x42

VIRGINIA MAHALEY THOMPSON
"Bells, Bells, Bells" (facing page)
Virginia Mahaley Thompson, Architect
Pen and ink 21x17

"Bells, Bells, Bells"

Virginia Mahaley Thompson

ED DELARA
Park Central Development (facing page)
Hellmuth, Obata & Kassabaum, P.C., Architects
Pen and ink, markers 36x60

WILLIAM E. NAST, AIA
Rock Island Dam, Wenatchee, Washington (above)
Stone & Webster, Architects & Engineers
Colored ink 26x18

MONA BROWN
The Bromley, Manhattan, New York
Philip Birnbaum & Associates, Architects
Pencil on illustration board 16x15

ERIC GOULD
Marshfield Hills, Marshfield, MA (above)
Huygens & DiMella, Architects
Prismacolor on print, 30x40

DAN RAIH, AIA
20/21 Custom House Street, Boston (right)
Bruner, Cott & Associates, Architects
Ink and colored pencil 30x36

ELIZABETH ANN DAY
The Wellington (facing page)
Jessen, Architect
Watercolor 20x15

MIGUELANGEL GUTTIERREZ
Restaurant (above)
Ink on mylar 42x30

BRENT E. BYERS, FAIA
The Ozark Building Lobby (right)
Corgan Associates, Architects
Prismacolor on vellum 18x18

JAMES LANDING   A PARENCORP DEVELOPMENT   HUYGENS & DIMELLA, INC. Architects and Planners

TERRY A. CRACKNELL
James Landing, Scituate, MA (above)
Huygens DiMella Shaffer & Associates, Architect
Watercolor on print 30x40

SHU-XIANG XI
Kenyon College Library (left)
Shepley, Bulfinch, Richardson & Abbott, Architects
Ink wash and Watercolor 24x36

Architecture In Perspective

II

Introduction

Steve Oles

Exhilarated and encouraged by the overwhelming public and professional response to the first Architecture in Perspective exhibition, and not too long after its success, the officers and supporters of ASAP began planning for Architecture in Perspective II. With the initiative of an impressed group of friends from Texas, together with a planned five-year program to cross the country, it was deemed time to "take the show on the road." Architecture in Perspective II was displayed from 1 October to 31 October 1987 at the LTV Pavilion in Dallas, Texas. Subsequent venues were in Washington, D.C., at the American Society of Civil Engineers and at the headquarters of the American Institute of Architects.

Jurors for the second annual competition were architectural illustrator Carlos Diniz of Los Angeles; University of Texas at Arlington Professor Richard Ferrier, AIA; and architect Hugh Newell Jacobsen, FAIA of Washington, D.C. The number of submissions swelled to five hundred thirty-six, from thirty-two states and Canadian provinces. From these, the jurors were to select approximately fifty for exhibition. Beginning with Architecture in Perspective II, the charge to the jurors became somewhat more specific. Selections could only include drawings which depicted "time-removed" projects—a building or environment, or a portion of a building not wholly existing at the time the drawing was made—i.e.: proposed architecture. Topographical drawings, made from observation of existing subject matter, were to be considered outside the realm of perspectivism. Rendered orthogonal drawings (elevations, plans, or sections) of time-removed designs were considered eligible for consideration even though linear perspective is technically absent from these works.

Juror Ferrier observed, "With rare exceptions, the drawings submitted were of very high caliber. It was apparent that we were selecting from a group of the most creative and proficient perspectivists currently in practice."

The actual jury process was conducted in Dallas in July 1987 and consisted of the progressive viewing and elimination of submitted works in slide format. Ferrier further commented, "The first cut was not difficult. However, it was problematic in that so few submissions were eliminated. Subsequent rounds stimulated considerable discussion. One of the determining criteria became well entrenched: was the image under consideration an exceptional example of the media and drawing type as well as a compelling presentation of the architecture? A concern...was evident in several submissions where the merits of the illustration exceeded that of the architecture being depicted."

The new criteria for selection notwithstanding, the single most profound difference between the first Architecture in Perspective competition and all those to follow occurred in 1987. This was the establishment of the profession's highest honor for excellence in the graphic representation of architecture—the Hugh Ferriss Memorial Prize, named in honor of the United State's best known architectural illustrator of the twentieth century. With an initial grant from the Van Nostrand Reinhold Company, the Ferriss Prize would be awarded annually to an individual whose work, in the opinion of that year's jury, was worthy of such

distinction. At the jury's discretion, the award, symbolized by a specially cast medallion, could be deferred if no selection attained the standard of excellence demanded by the Ferriss legacy.

The winner of the first annual Hugh Ferriss Memorial Prize was Richard Lovelace of Boston. The jury deliberations were succinctly encapsulated by juror Hugh Newell Jacobsen: "The 1987 ASAP jury was unanimous in its selection of this year's recipient of the Hugh Ferriss Memorial Prize."

"Rendering," as Mr. Ferriss himself wrote in 1940, "is a means toward an end; the end is architecture." With the establishment of this award, the American Society of Architectural Perspectivists intended to provide a most desirable impetus not only to higher standards in the graphic representation of architecture but to higher standards of achievement in the field of architecture itself.

ARCHITECTURE IN PERSPECTIVE II 1987
Jurors Diniz, Ferrier, and Jacobsen (facing page)

The Hugh Ferriss Memorial Prize

The recipient of the first annual Hugh Ferriss Memorial Prize was Richard Lovelace of Boston for his engaging, masterful pencil drawing entitled "One Montvale Avenue," a portion of a proposed Massachusetts office building. The award was conferred in Dallas at celebrations attendant to the exhibition, Architecture in Perspective II.

Without question, Hugh Ferriss (1889-1962) was this nation's most celebrated and influential architectural illustrator. Born in St. Louis and trained as an architect, Ferriss elected to draw rather than to build. He nevertheless perceived his role as a formgiver and theorist. His powerfully romantic visions of utopian urban life—both single structures and entire cityscape—would serve as more than inspiration to generations of architects and artists. They proved to be highly instrumental in shaping much of what was to become the best of that era's modern architecture. Ferriss defined the art of renderings as "an attempt to tell the truth about a building." This idea of truth, however, was more than the simple reporting of structural "facts:" it included the equally important component of "interpretation." In the words of Ferriss, "Buildings possess an individual existence, varying—now dynamic, now serene—but vital, as all else in the universe."

Mr. Lovelace's winning piece was described by *The Dallas Morning News* architecture critic David Dillion as "enigmatic…a suburban office building seen—viewer's choice—from inside out or outside in." Juror Ferrier wrote: "The 'One Montvale Avenue' drawing was so powerful that discussion was not required. It was the unanimous selection for the Ferriss Award." And in the words of juror Jacobson: "The drawing at once expresses the skill and spirit so evocative of the honored work of Mr. Ferriss. Not only does the perspective dramatically describe the project at its potential best, but fires the imagination of the viewer in tandem with the concept of the architect."

The elemental, planar description of space, articulated by the muted contrast of an evening atmosphere, is nonetheless sensitively enhanced by the effusive glow of an illuminated interior. Given Mr. Lovelace's training as an architect, and his affinity for drawing, he was fired, no doubt, by the aesthetic of Mr. Ferriss. Further examples of Mr. Lovelace's inspired work can be found in subsequent chapters.

RICHARD LOVELACE
One Montvale Avenue, Stoneham, MA
August Associates, Architects
Wax-based pencil on vellum 16x14

Selected Entries

MARC PARTRIDGE
Urban Masterplan, Helmet, CA (right)
Marc Partridge & Nick Marcucci, Architects
Airbrush on photocopy 20x20

GILBERT GORSKI, AIA
Riverwalk for Cityfront Center, Chicago (below)
Lohan Associates, Architects
Watercolor 11x17

ELIZABETH ANN DAY
Mellon Bank, Philadelphia (facing page)
Kohn, Pedersen, Fox Associates, Architects
Watercolor 13x11

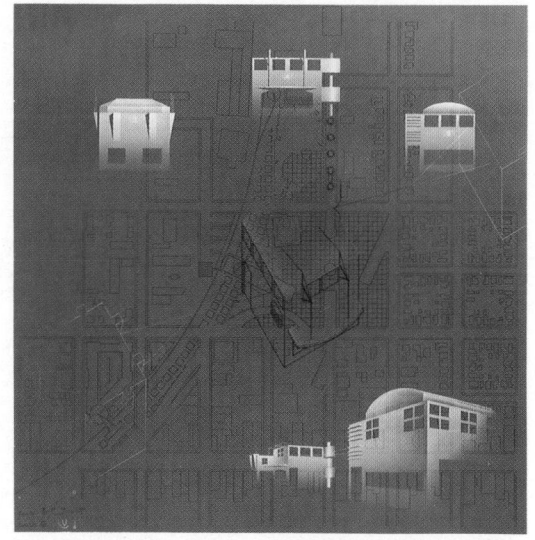

FRANK M. COSTANTINO
176 Federal Street, Boston
August Associates, Architects
Pencil on vellum 11x14

FRANK M. COSTANTINO
Becton Dickinson, Franklin Lakes, NJ (above)
Kallmann, McKinnell & Wood, Architects
Pencil 30x40

FRANK M. COSTANTINO
Peabody Museum, Salem, MA (right)
Kallmann, McKinnell & Wood, Architects
Film lead on paper 12x16

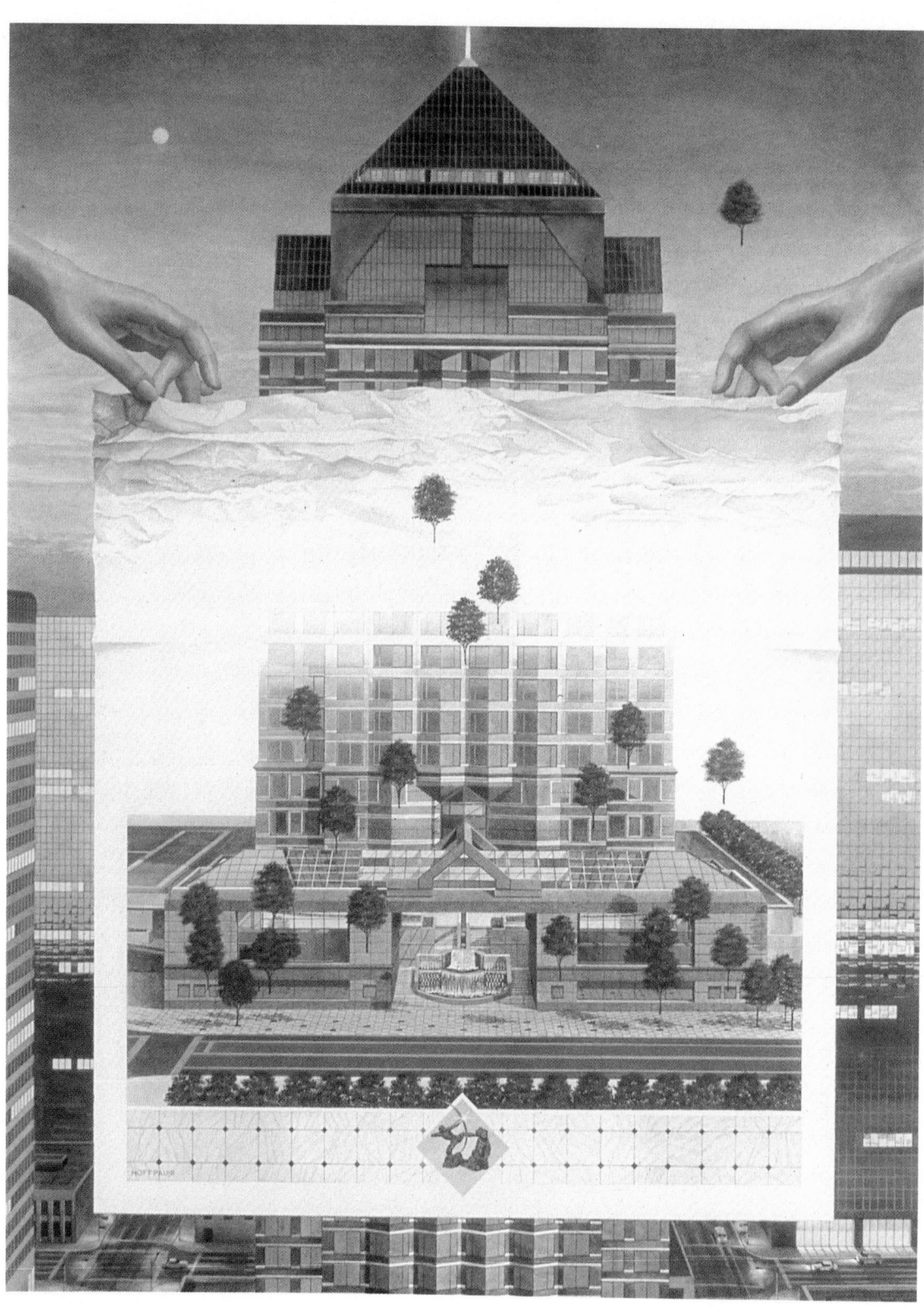

HOFFPAUIR/ROSNER STUDIO
LTV Tower, Dallas (facing page)
Skidmore, Owings & Merrill, Architects
Mixed media 40x30

MIGUELANGEL GUTIERREZ
Dallas Main Center, Dallas (right)
JPJ Architects
Watercolor and airbrush 22x28

JAMES TURNER
Broadway Beautification, Galveston, Texas (below)
Scott Slaney & Slaney Santana Group, Architects
Watercolor 30x40

W. DAVID SHAW
Outdoor Livingroom (above)
Acrylic on illustration board 14x21

RAEL D. SLUTSKY
75 State Street, Boston (left)
Skidmore, Owings & Merrill and Graham Gund, Architects
Pen and ink with color pencils 24x18

RAEL D. SLUTSKY
75 State Street, Boston (facing page)
Skidmore, Owings & Merrill and Graham Gund, Architects
Pen and ink with color pencils 27x14

MONGKOL TANSANTISUK
 AT&T Corporate Headquarters, Chicago (facing page)
Skidmore, Owings & Merrill, Architects
Wax-based pencil 11x17

MONGKOL TANSANTISUK
Vanderbilt University, Nashville, TN (above)
The Stubbins Associates, Architects
Wax-based pencil 17x10

MONGKOL TANSANTISUK
Roseland III, Roseland, NJ (right)
The Stubbins Associates, Architects
Wax-based pencil 17x11

SHU-XIANG XI
Smithsonian Institution, Kiosk, Washington, DC
Shepley, Bulfinch, Richardson & Abbott, Architects
Ink brush with color 30x30

ANDREW HICKES
Plaza at Rio Condominiums, New York (above)
The Gruzen Partnership, Architects
Airbrush and ink 30x40

ANDREW HICKES
Transpotomac Canal Center, Washington, DC (right)
CHK Architects & Planners, Architects
Airbrush and ink 30x40

THOMAS SCHALLER
Judiciary Office Building, Washington, DC (above)
Kohn, Pedersen, Fox Associates, Architects
Watercolor 32x48

RICHARD C. MEYER
Boathouse, St. Andrew's School, Middleton, Delaware (left)
Richard C. Meyer, Architect
Pen and ink 11x17

THOMAS SCHALLER
125 Summer Street, Boston (facing page)
Kohn, Pedersen, Fox Associates, Architects
Watercolor 40x30

ROBERT FRANK
Cinema 7, Pasadena, CA (facing page)
The Ehrenkrantz Group, Architects
Pencil on board 13x11

SYDNEY MEAD
"L.A. 2015" (above)
Sydney Mead, Designer
Gouche 20x30

STEFAN A. TRENDOV
Minnesota Historical Building, St. Paul (right)
Rapson/TAC/Stageberg, Architects
Ink and graphite 32x36

ROBERT W. COOK
Poydras Square Shopping Center, New Orleans (above)
Hellmuth, Obata & Kassabaum, P.C., Architects
Gouche 20x30

ROBERT W. COOK
McKinney, Monticello Office, Dallas (left)
Harwood K. Smith Associates, Architects
Gouche 14x24

ROBERT COMAZZI
Exeter Street Theater, Boston
Developmental Resources, Architects
Watercolor 24x26

SUNS HUNG
The Rizzoli Building, New York (facing page)
Kohn, Pedersen, Fox Associates, Architects
Airbrush 32x23

MICHAEL REARDON
Woodmark Hotel, Sunnyvale, CA (above)
Frizzell Hill Moorhouse Architects
Ink and watercolor 12x24

SUNS HUNG
Three Park Avenue, New York (right)
Shreve, Lamb, Ambersand & Harmon, Architects
Airbrush 30x18

DONGIK LEE
Austin City Hall Complex, Austin, TX (above)
Black Atkinson Vernooy, Architects
Watercolor with pen and ink 20x24

DONGIK LEE
Austin Nature Center, TX (left)
Black Atkinson Vernooy, Architects
Watercolor with pen and ink 13x33

STANLEY DOCTOR
Colorado Gateway Convention Center, Denver (facing page)
I.M. Pei & Partners, Architects
Prismacolor and watercolor 40x32

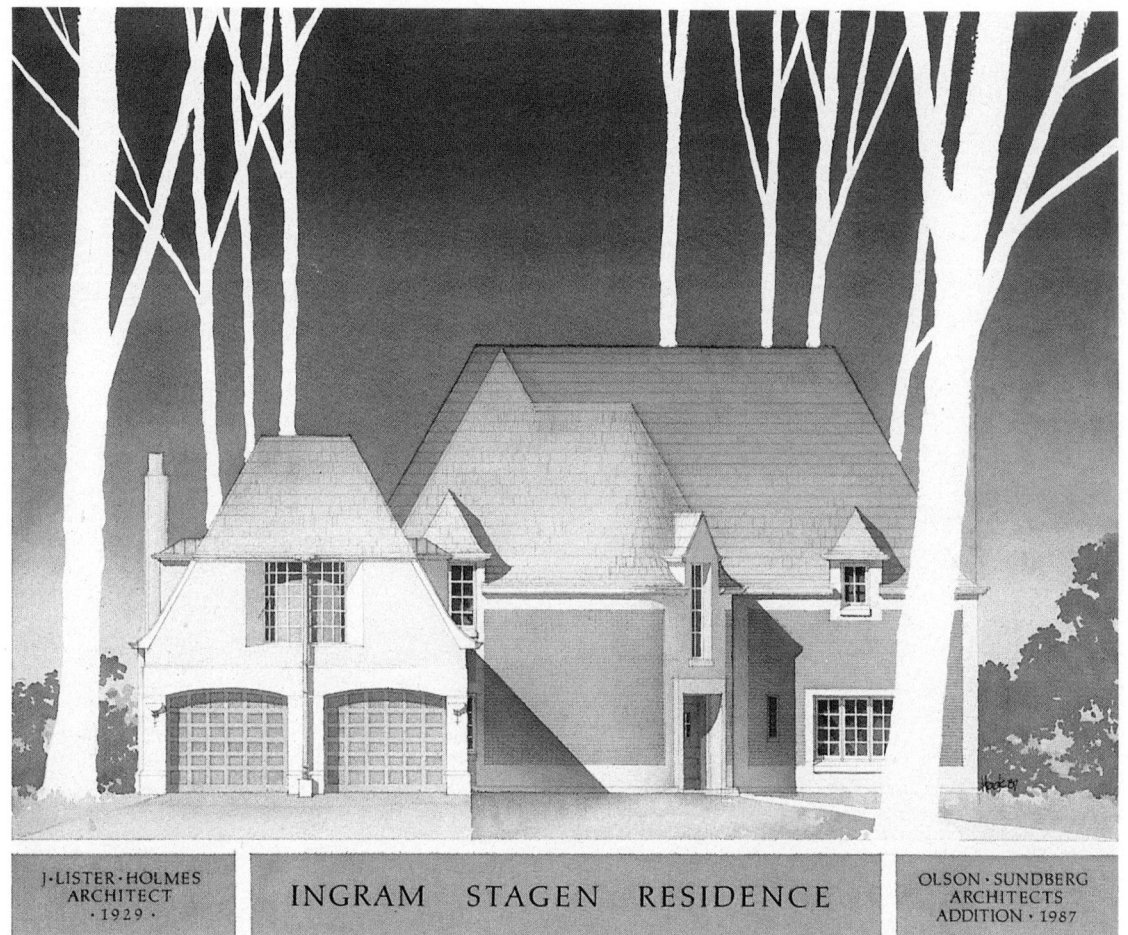

J·LISTER·HOLMES ARCHITECT ·1929·

INGRAM STAGEN RESIDENCE

OLSON·SUNDBERG ARCHITECTS ADDITION·1987

WILLIAM HOOK
Ingram Stagen Residence, Seattle (above)
Olson Sundberg Architects
Watercolor 16x20

BRENT E. BYERS, FAIA
Old City Jail, Dallas (left)
Corgan Associates, Architects
Prismacolor 17x22

BRENT E. BYERS, FAIA
Dallas Ballet
Corgan Associates, Architects
Prismacolor 26x19

BRIAN FISHER & RICHARD POLING
Hibiscus House, Florida (above)
Andres Duany & Elizabeth Plater-Zyberk, Architects
Gouche 31x28

STEPHEN S. EVANUSA, AIA
Bryan Residence, Maryland (left)
Hugh Newell Jacobsen, FAIA, Architects
Ink on mylar 20x30

STEPHEN S. EVANUSA
Adirondack Residence, Bolton, NY
Stephen S. Evanusa, AIA, Architect
Ink on mylar 30x20

RICHARD LOVELACE
Erie Community College, Buffalo, NY (above)
Cannon Design, Architects
Wax-based pencil on vellum 16x24

DEAN B. LEWIS
"The Overlook" (left)
Dean B. Lewis, Architect
Prismacolor on vellum 20x30

ERNEST BURDEN, III
Faison Building, Charlotte, NC (facing page)
Kohn, Pedersen, Fox Associates, Architects
Mixed media 24x16

MONA BROWN
City Hall Competition, The Hague, Holland (above)
Richard Meier & Partners, Architects
Wax-based pencil on black board 26x26

WENDY E. EVANS, AIA
Holocaust Memorial Museum, Washington, DC (left)
I.M. Pei & Partners, Architects
Pencil on mylar 12x16

PETER A.G. ROPER
Hydro Quebec Competition, Montreal
Joboin Lamarre Pratt, Architects
Prismacolor on blackline 42x30

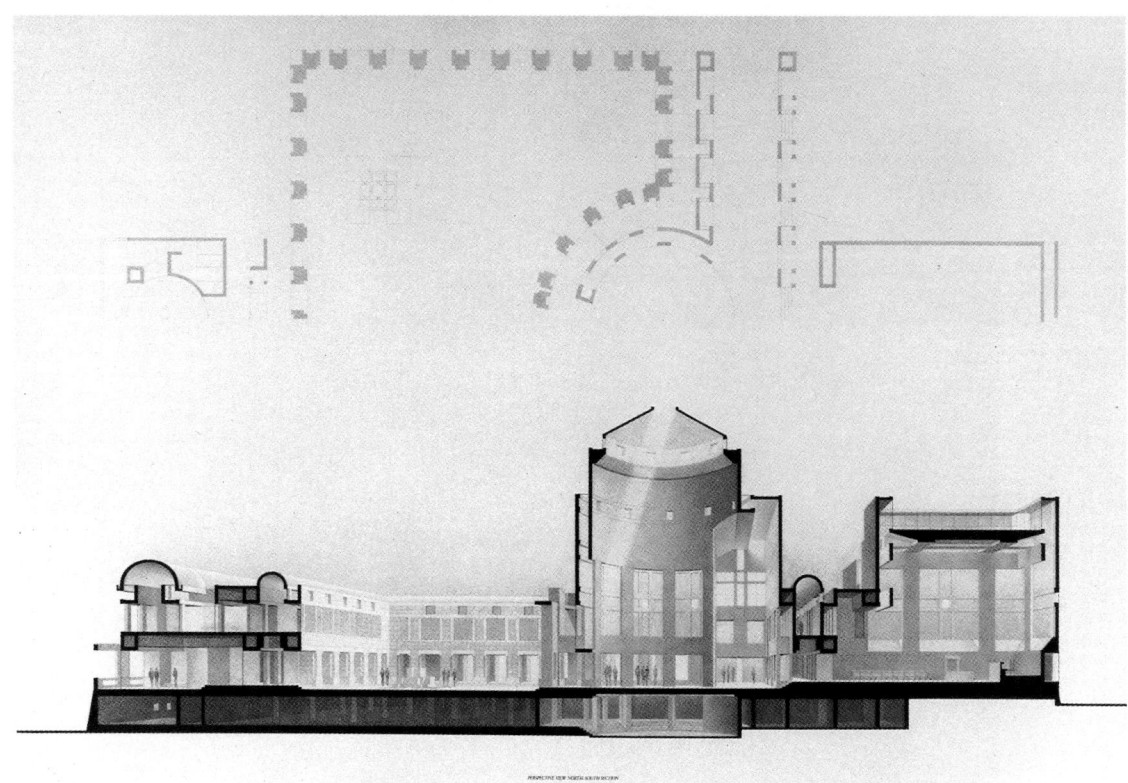

MONA BROWN
Supreme Court Competition, Jerusalem
I.M. Pei & Partners, Architects
Prismacolor and ink 30x40

Architecture In Perspective

III

Introduction

Steve Oles

Architecture in Perspective III premiered at the Pacific Design Center in Los Angeles, California on 7 October 1988. As the sphere of influence of the American Society of Architectural Perspectivists and interest in its activities (especially the annual competition) continued to expand, venues were added to what had become a genuine travelling exhibition. Following the close of the Los Angeles show, Architecture in Perspective III appeared in four locations throughout 1988 and 1989. These were respectively, the San Francisco Chapter of the A.I.A.; the Portland, Oregon Chapter of the A.I.A.; the Minneapolis, Minnesota Society of the A.I.A.; and the National Convention of the A.I.A. in St. Louis, Missouri in May 1989.

As before, three notable design professionals accepted the invitation to serve as jurors for the event. They were architect Charles Bassett, FAIA, of San Francisco, California; Dean Emeritus Ralph Rapson, FAIA, of the University of Minnesota; and architectural delineator Barry Zauss of Los Angeles. Four hundred sixty-three works from artists across the United States and Canada were submitted for the jury's consideration. No significant changes in the previous year's juror guidelines were made—entrants' work must be of proposed architecture only. No drawings of wholly extant architecture would be accepted. As in past years, to maintain a consistent and fair evaluation, entrants' work (a maximum of five submissions per individual) was judged in slide format only. No photographic prints or original drawings could be entered, given the large number of submitted pieces. The judging procedure for Architecture in Perspective III differed, however, from the back-breaking process of earlier years by eliminating the use of a light box. All work, even in the initial rounds, was seen by projection only. Following an intensive day of deliberations in June of 1988 at the offices of ASAP advisory councillor Carlos Diniz, a total of forty-six works were identified and deemed worthy of exhibition.

Mr. Bassett, jury chairman, wrote: "The jury was impressed by the very high standard set by all entries. Judging two drawings of similar technique and accomplishment was difficult; in such cases we always chose that piece whose particular qualities would contribute most to an exhibit of the greatest diversity and richness. Several drawings were superb examples of what happens when an artist's talent and perception of a problem mesh perfectly in method and mood to the needs of the subject."

Professional illustrator and juror Zauss expressed his delight at the range of style and technique. He stated his criteria for the selection of exhibit-worthy pieces as: "1. A well-constructed perspective and composition, possibly including controlled distortion. 2. Value pattern and color designed to focus attention on the subject matter in an interesting way. 3. Well-executed technique. 4. Character. In exceptional cases, a rendering may convey a feeling that lifts it above the norm."

Following lengthy deliberations due to the unusually high numbers and overall quality of the submissions, the second annual Hugh Ferriss Memorial Prize was awarded to architect/artist Thomas Schaller of New York City for a water-color rendition of one of his own designs entitled "Proposed Arts and Cultural Center, Rome." Schaller was presented the Ferriss Prize medallion on 8 October 1988 at the ASAP awards ceremony in Los Angeles.

Beyond doubt, Architecture in Perspective III was convincing proof that ASAP was alive and well. The range of support and interest continued to grow. An Advisory Council staff was expanded to include representation from ten states; with increasing interest from other countries, International Coordinators were appointed to link the efforts of ASAP with like-minded colleagues in Great Britain, Japan, China, Australia, and, of course, Canada. In his concluding comments, jury chairman Bassett commended "...the members of ASAP; the quality and number of submissions attest to a lively and continuing tradition of fine architectural draughtsmanship in North America."

ARCHITECTURE IN PERSPECTIVE III 1988
Jurors Zauss, Rapson, and Bassett (facing page)

WILBUR PEARSON
Tequesta Cove, Florida (above)
John J. Sklanka, Architect
Pencil on vellum 17x23

MICHAEL ELAVSKY
University of Notre Dame, Indiana (left)
Ellerbe, Becket, Architects
Marker and pencil on blackline 15x15

MICHAEL ELAVSKY
ConAgra Headquarters
Opus Corporation, Architects
Ink on mylar 19x19

T. KELLY WILSON
The Pru, Great Galleria, Boston (facing page)
Frederick Koetter, Architect
Pencil on Strathmore 21x18

MICHAEL SECHMAN
First and Mission, San Francisco (right)
Skidmore, Owings & Merrill, Architects
Pencil on vellum 15x14

T. KELLY WILSON
1-2-3 Center Plaza, Boston (below)
Schwartz, Silver, Architects
Pencil on Strathmore 16x32

DAVID M. LANE
The Base, Telluride, Colorado (above)
Wheeler, Piper, Architects
Mixed media 24x36

MICHAEL McCANN
Peaks Competition, Hong Kong (left)
Douglas Muir, Architect
Watercolor 15x22

MICHAEL McCANN
Protypical Atrium Space (facing page)
Michael McCann, Designer
Watercolor 21x35

RAEL D. SLUTSKY
One Liberty Place, Philadelphia (facing page)
Murphy/Jahn, Architects
Pen and ink with color pencils 30x18

RAEL D. SLUTSKY
One North Franklin Street, Chicago (right)
Skidmore, Owings & Merrill, Architects
Pen and ink with color pencils 40x20

RAEL D. SLUTSKY
Bishops Gate, London (below)
Skidmore, Owings & Merrill, Architects
Pen and ink with color pencils 18x25

CARLOS DINIZ & ASSOCIATES
Canary Wharf, London (above)
Skidmore, Owings & Merrill, Architects
Mixed media 33x44

TERRY CRACKNELL
Residence, Scottsdale Arizona (left)
Huygens & DiMella, Architects
Pencil on pebbly sepia 10x24

RICHARD BERGMANN, FAIA
St. Michael's Lutheran Church (facing page)
Richard Bergmann, FAIA, Architect
Pen and ink 40x30

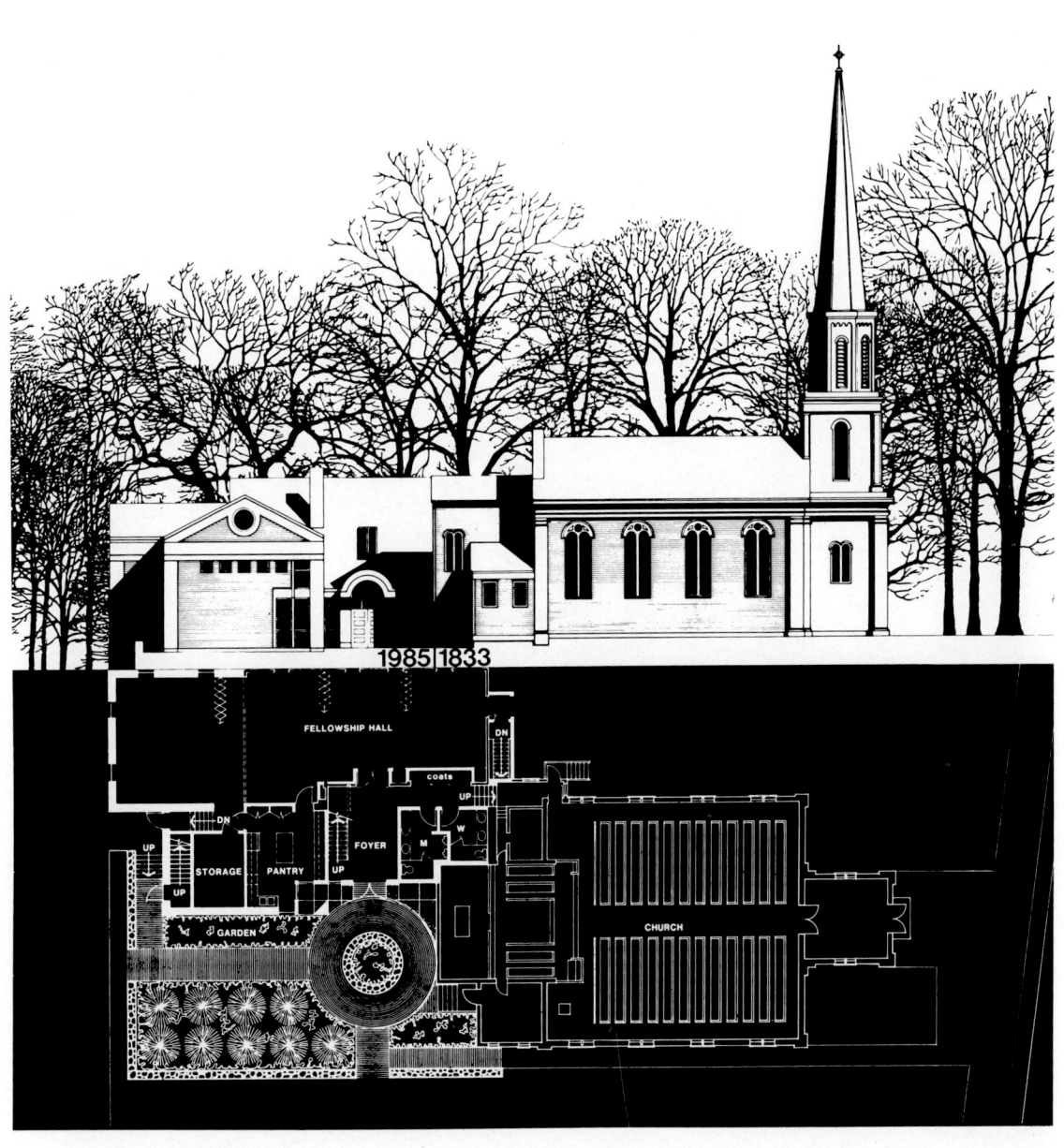

1985 1833

FELLOWSHIP HALL

coats

DN

UP

FOYER

DN

M W

UP

STORAGE

PANTRY

UP

CHURCH

UP

GARDEN

HOFFPAUIR/ROSNER STUDIO
Memphis Brooks Museum, Memphis, TN (facing page)
Skidmore, Owings & Merrill, Architects
Watercolor 38x28

RICHARD LOVELACE
Winter Garden, Waterfront Competition, NY (above)
Richard Lovelace, Designer
Charcoal pencil on tracing paper 8x10

RICHARD LOVELACE
The Lagoon, Waterfront Competition, NY (right)
Richard Lovelace, Designer
Charcoal pencil on tracing paper 8x10

CHRISTOPHER GRUBBS
Hyatt Fantasy Resort (above)
Gail S. Grant, Architect
Prismacolor on paper 10x15

CHRISTOPHER GRUBBS
California State University Competition (left)
The Architects Collaborative, Architects
Prismacolor on paper 13x20

ELIZABETH H. SULLIVAN
Residence, Sherborn, MA (facing page)
Richard Puffer, Architect
Pencil and airbrush on paper 24x18

125 MILL STREET • SHERBORN • MA

MICHAEL REARDON
Waterfront Plan, San Francisco
ROMA Design Group, Architects
Ink on mylar 40x40

ANTOINE PREDOCK, FAIA
Fine Arts Complex, Arizona State University (above)
Antoine Predock, FAIA, Architect
Pastels 8x10

ANTOINE PREDOCK, FAIA
Fine Arts Complex, Arizona State University (right)
Antoine Predock, FAIA, Architect
Pastels 8x10

ROBERT McILHARGEY
St. Lawrence Market Complex, Toronto (above)
Holston Bakker, Architects
Mixed media 17x24

BARBARA RATNER
Bellsouth Services Headquarters (left)
Cooper Carry & Associates, Architects
Prismacolor 10x18

DAN HARMON
400 Peachtree, Atlanta (facing page)
John Portman & Associates, Architects
Ink and airbrush 72x36

WILLIAM G. HOOK
Franklin High School, Seattle (above)
Bassetti, Norton, Metler, Rekevics, Architects
Watercolor 24x36

WILLIAM G. HOOK
Centrum Performance Center, Washington (left)
The Bumgardner Architects
Watercolor 20x30

RICHARD C. BAEHR
Williamsburg Bridge, New York (facing page)
Amman & Whitney, Architects & Engineers
Tempera 27x17

FRANK BARTUS
University of South Florida, Orlando (above)
VOA Associates, Architects
Gouache and airbrush 14x23

JAMES HADLEY
Round Hill Estate, West Indies (left)
Gaudy-Hadley Associates, Architects
Stylist nylon-tipped pen 11x16

ELIZABETH ANN DAY
Mellon Bank, Philadelphia (facing page)
Kohn, Pedersen, Fox Associates, Architects
Watercolor 13x13

FRANK M. COSTANTINO
Main Aquarium Tank, Osaka, Japan (above)
Cambridge Seven Associates, Architects
Watercolor 18x12

JOHN BLOOD
Museum of Ansel Adams Photographs, CA (left)
John Blood, Architects
Pencil on paper 11x12

FRANK M. COSTANTINO
Pier Four, Boston (facing page)
Kallmann, McKinnell & Wood, Architects
Pencil on paper 14x12

JAMES GARLAND
Johnson Residence, Racine, Wisconsin (above)
Charles Moore, FAIA, Architect
Watercolor and ink 22x30

MICHAEL GURAN
The Courtyards, Naples, FL (left)
Benjamin Thompson & Associates, Architects
Chalk on yellow trace 19x23

Architecture In Perspective
IV

Introduction

Steve Oles

No less venerable a location than The Art Institute of Chicago hosted the premiere of Architecture in Perspective IV on 6 October 1989. Subsequent venues included Detroit's Lawrence Institute of Technology, Lansing's Northern Michigan University, Toronto's Aird Gallery, Ontario, Canada and the A.I.A. Convention in Houston.

The jury for Architecture in Perspective IV was chaired by Yale Architecture Dean Thomas H. Beeby and also included Joseph Gonzalez, general partner at SOM/Chicago and Pauline Saliga, Assistant Curator of Architecture at The Art Institute of Chicago. The jury's task was made all the more daunting in light of the record number of entries—no fewer than five hundred sixty slides. The intensive day-long process occurred in June 1989 at the Chicago offices of ASAP advisory councillor Rael Slutsky, and eventually, after arduous deliberations, fifty-nine exceptional pieces emerged for inclusion in the exhibition. The selected works were also illustrative of the extended membership base of ASAP, with representative drawings from across the United States, Canada and Mexico—a truly North American showing.

A significant evolution of the awards-selection process was evidenced in 1989 for Architecture in Perspective IV. Recognizing the vast disparity of intellectual and technical approaches to diverse methods of architectural graphic representation, the executive board of ASAP established two separate categories for entry in the competition. Category "A" was for finished presentation drawings of proposed architecture, while the broader, less defined Category "B" was for conceptual drawings and sketches. It was intended that these categories would encourage entrants to submit drawings at any level of "finish" or architectural specificity.

To quote juror Saliga, "The ancient Chinese saying, 'May you live in interesting times,' is an appropriate sentiment for anyone interested in the current production of professional architectural renderings. Never before has there been such freedom to experiment with style and technique; never has there been such diversity in personal approaches to depicting architecture on a two-dimensional surface. As the drawings that have been chosen for the Architecture in Perspective exhibitions of the past five years demonstrate, the varied materials of airbrushed ink, charcoal, acrylic paint, watercolor, and the common pencil have been cleverly utilized to transform blank canvases, paper, rag board, Mylar, and other surfaces into magical renderings of unequalled diversity and quality."

"The jury was pleased to see the numbers, quality, and variety in this year's submissions," wrote Juror Beeby. "Drawings were evident from artists commissioned to illustrate others' work to architects representing their own buildings to conceptual works exploring architectural ideas. There was a clear tendency, which makes sense in this context, to push the works beyond conventional realism. Superrealistic and surrealistic impulses propelled many drawings toward iconography and techniques visible in recent and not-so-recent art."

"Humor, drama, surrealism are among the characteristics represented in the Architecture in Perspective IV exhibit that I was privileged to jury," stated Ms. Saliga. It is surely no surprise to find many of those characteristics suffused in the winning work by Daniel Willis. His romantic rendition was awarded the third annual Hugh Ferriss Memorial Prize in ceremonies at The Art Institute of Chicago on 6 October 1989.

Other awards presented that evening were "Best in Category A," to architect Jonathan Levi of Brookline, Massachusetts and "Best in Category B," to artist/illustrator Chris Anderson of New York City. In addition, three "Juror Awards" were bestowed upon works by Gilbert Gorski of Chicago, Rael Slutsky of Chicago and Holt Hinshaw Pfau and Jones of San Francisco. The words of jury chair Beeby were an appropriate summation of the process: "The Jury would like to commend all the entrants for the clear intensity and energy that this year's submission so obviously displayed. We all look forward to the results of future…competitions that have grown so rapidly into an event of major significance."

ARCHITECTURE IN PERSPECTIVE IV 1989
Jurors Beeby, Saliga, and Gonzalez (facing page)

The Hugh Ferriss Memorial Prize

The Art Institute of Chicago was the setting for the presentation of the third annual Hugh Ferriss Memorial Prize to architect and Penn State assistant professor of architecture Daniel Willis for a beautiful pencil work entitled "Edgar Allan Poe Memorial." The piece was one of the more conceptual works among the submissions.

It was the intent of the work, in the words of Willis, "...to illustrate the passing of time, which progresses from left to right in the rendering. The Gothic wall (inspired by Poe's story, *Masque of Red Death*) is relatively new at the far left, and several hundred years old at the far right." Poe's fascination with time's corrosive effects on objects and life has led Willis to create a two-dimensional drawing which implies not only the spatial (third) dimension, but the temporal (fourth) as well.

Willis further explained: "The drawing attempts to capture some of the mystery of Poe's work, and to explore themes of decay and material change. I thought that pencil was the appropriate medium, for the 'depth' it allows one to produce in the drawing." The memorial to Poe is a theoretical project that Mr. Willis has been developing for several years. It remains, in fact, an ongoing process. Willis has also been exploring ideas of time progression and how they might be graphically portrayed through the use of reflections in water. He notes that Poe, Lewis Carroll,

and many other writers have used reflections as windows that reveal other realities.

The eternal, engaging mystery of fleeting time remains a challenging enigma to an architect's visionary and representational skills. Mr. Willis' controlled, almost pastel-like, pencil work is crisp and descriptive (nearly effecting a flat, graphic pattern), on the left foreground, and subtly diffuses to a suggestive tonal depiction on the right background. The message of his drawing seems to invite us to project our imaginations beyond his facile illustration of this symbolic form to a contemplation of the temporal concept. In any case, this work is certainly a clear indication that the exploration of architectural evolution and theory is very much the artist's province.

DANIEL E. WILLIS
Edgar Allan Poe Memorial (facing page)
Daniel E. Willis, Architect
Pencil 30x20

Category "A" Award

JONATHAN LEVI
Residence in Boylston, MA
Jonathan Levi, Architect
Watercolor 25x56

Introduced for the 1989 competition, the American Society of Architectural Perspectivists established an expanded awards program—offering not only the Hugh Ferriss Memorial Prize but also recognition of other works—to further encourage entries as diverse, imaginative, innovative, or visionary as possible. The first winner of the newly established ASAP award for "Best in Category 'A'—Finished Presentation Drawings" was Jonathan Levi of Brookline, Massachusetts, for a most impressive (and impressively large) watercolor rendition of a private residence in Massachusetts. The delicately hued but nonetheless powerful work possessed a distinctly impressionistic and ethereal quality, and in Mr. Levi's words, "…describes the occupation of an idealized natural landscape by a simple architectural figure in repose. However, the true subject of the painting is the luminous ether of space which binds the two together—making tangible the illusion of place and time."

Category "B" Award

The intended purpose of a "Best in Category 'B'—Conceptual Drawings and Sketches" in the 1989 Architecture in Perspective IV competition was to encourage the submittal of both the looser, evocative sketch or design process drawings, as well as more strictly imaginative, conceptual or exploratory work at any level of finish.

Chris Anderson of New York City, as the first winner in the new category, was a fitting recipient. Her "Proposal for an Idaho Farmhouse (The Row House)" is a powerful expression, in black-and-white oil on canvas, of the tension between the here and now, and the infinite, the mundane, and the surreal. The work, in Ms. Anderson's words, "was a house form conceived for an archetypal site which I call the 'margin of tension,' the place where suburbia meets rural America. The painting is part of an ongoing body of work which explores the dynamics of America's changing geographic and cultural landscape."

CHRIS ANDERSON*
Proposal for an Idaho Farmhouse (The Row House)
Chris Anderson, Designer
Oil and charcoal 48x72

Juror Award

GILBERT GORSKI, AIA
181 Madison Building, Chicago
Cesar Pelli & Associates, Architects
Prismacolor 27x16

An unusually dramatic Prismacolor pencil view by Gilbert Gorski of a Chicago office-building proposal designed by Cesar Pelli and Associates received a 1989 AIP IV Juror Award .

A carefully articulated study of architectural forms and specific material depiction, the work nevertheless simultaneously succeeds in conveying a convincing and inspiring sense of the effects of light and the soaring reach of classic skyscraper design. Lighting and color usage seem particularly fortuitous but no more so than the rarely utilized, yet entirely appropriate, angle of view. Also quite successful is the close-cropped partial view of the tower, which adds drama by absorbing the viewer into the work.

This drawing is a good example of a solution to the perspectivist's constant dilemma of generating a highly realistic image while simultaneously attempting to infuse that image with an interpretive aesthetic quality. It is this gifted artist's use of three-point perspective, in tandem with the sensitive application of color, which truly affords the viewer not only a sense of what "181 Madison Building" might look like, but how it might actually feel to be there. Mr. Gorski's work is clear proof that there is no adequate substitute for the talents of the architectural perspectivist in attempting to tell the truth about a proposed building.

Juror Award

Their own design proposal for a warden's house at Alcatraz provided celebrated San Francisco-based architects Holt Hinshaw Pfau Jones with a canvas for the remarkable image which garnered their 1989 IV Juror Award.

The work may at first seem to be a deceptively simple and straightforward application of ink-line drawing shaded with gray Zip-a-Tone paper, but is at the end a surprisingly sophisticated and complex composition of shapes and shades. The piece, which depicts a detail of an elevation of the project, is at once uncompromisingly "modern" and yet reminiscent of the formal Beaux-Arts elevational ink-wash drawings of the early 1800s. As in those much-admired works of earlier days, there seems to be nothing in this modern composition that is unnecessary—everything is there for a reason. The depiction of the materials and the effects of light (including reflections in the glass planes) are all here, but in proper proportion, given proper importance, and orchestrated into a harmonious whole.

There is, in fact, a strictness and discipline in both the proposed design (perhaps owing to its intended purpose) and the presentation technique which is not at all at odds with the rigid formality of Beaux-Arts didactics. As figurative composition, there is a great economy and clarity in the visual information provided—materials, shade, and shadow. As pure abstraction, the rich play of dark and light, solid and void, make this an unusually compelling image.

HOLT HINSHAW PFAU JONES
Warden's House, Alcatraz, CA
Holt Hinshaw Pfau Jones, Architects
Ink and Zip-a-tone 30x30

Juror Award

RAEL D. SLUTSKY
Bishopgate Phase 9/10, London
Skidmore, Owings & Merrill, Architects
Pen and ink with color pencils 18x26

Rael Slutsky's wonderfully comprehensive and deft treatment of a proposed entry space for a Skidmore, Owings & Merrill project in London was a most deserving choice for a 1989 Juror Award. The space within the point of view of the drawing is accurately and faithfully depicted but the choice to reflect the curved space behind the viewer in the glass wall was inspired.

Mr. Slutsky explained his approach: "The loggia entry space is richly detailed in concrete, marble, granite, and polished metal. The renderer visually reinforced the space by treating the glass lobby wall as partly reflective and partly transparent. The curving, converging arcade behind the viewer is reflected in the glass. A glimpse into the lobby shows how the detailing is translated into wood paneling surfaces. A hint of street activity and neighboring buildings provides context." The compositional complexities of such a space were carefully planned and expertly executed in the difficult medium of pen-and-ink. Color was subsequently added in this two-stage process.

Selected Entries

SARAH BRANNEN
Winter Garden, Beal Office Building, Waltham, MA
Jung/Brannen & Associates, Architects
Watercolor 27x24

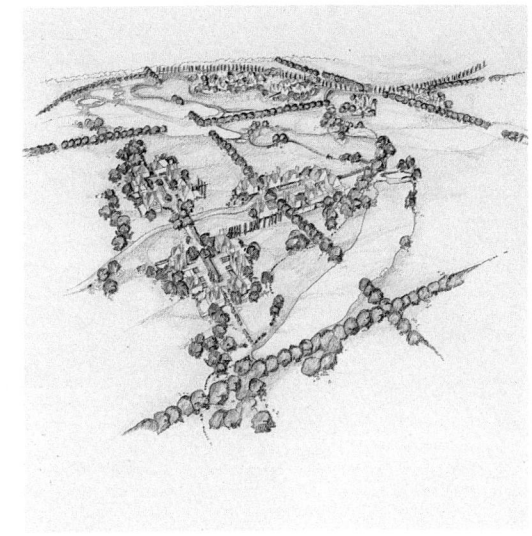

BENJAMIN C. PILCHARD*
The Conclusion of an Era...? (facing page)
Benjamin C. Pilchard, Architect
Charcoal 30x24

STANLEY DOCTOR
Townhouses at Beaver Creek, CO (above)
Gordon Pierce & Associates, Architects
Colored pencil and gouche 24x36

STEPHEN SIEGLE
Conway Farms South, Chicago (right)
Booth/Hansen & Associates, Architect
Colored pencil 22x30

WILBUR PEARSON
Hinkle Residence, Florida (above)
Ken Tate, Architect
Pencil on vellum 18x24

RICHARD FERRIER, AIA*
Windows and Fragments: Narrative Visions (right)
Richard Ferrier, AIA, Architect
Mixed media 22x30

RICHARD LOVELACE*
Civic Plaza and Office Towers, New York
Beyer, Blinder & Belle, Architects
Charcoal pencil on tracing paper 8x8

GILBERT GORSKI, AIA*
The Baths of Schaumburg (facing page)
Gilbert Gorski, AIA Architect
Prismacolor 30x20

ROBERT McILHARGEY
Expo '92, Seville, Spain (right)
Expo '92 Planning Department, Architects
Mixed media 39x39

BARBARA RATNER
Pier 66 Master Development Plan, Florida (below)
Cooper, Carry & Associates, Architects
Acrylic 20x24

STEWART WHITE
1629 Connecticut Avenue, Washington, DC
Wiebenson & Associates, Architects
Watercolor and pastel 22x20

THOMAS NORMAN RAJKOVICH*
Chicago Waterworks Tower (above)
Thomas Norman Rajkovich, Architect
Pen and ink on museum board 31x15

RAEL D. SLUTSKY
100 North Riverside, Chicago (right)
Perkins & Will, Architects
Pen and ink with color pencils 36x12

TAMOTSU YAMAMOTO*
Charles River, Boston (above)
Tamotsu Yamamoto, Designer
Color pencil 36x84

MONA BROWN
Convention Center, Los Angeles (left)
I.M. Pei & Partners, Architects
Prismacolor on museum board 10x14

MARK CROW
Residential Interior (facing page)
Mark Crow, Architect
Mixed media 32x30

THOMAS SCHALLER
Dominus Winery, California (above)
I.M. Pei & Partners, Architects
Watercolor 22x30

BRUCE BONDY*
Galati Tower, Beaver Island, Michigan (left)
Decker & Kemp, Architects
Pen and ink on vellum 17x15

THOMAS SCHALLER
Proposed Archaeology Museum, Crete (facing page)
Thomas Schaller, Architect
Watercolor 22x17

HOFFPAUIR/ROSNER STUDIO
Memphis Brooks Museum of Art, Memphis, TN (left)
Skidmore, Owings & Merrill, Architects
Ink wash 26x26

THOMAS A. SPAIN
Mark and Bonnie Blank Residence (below)
Thomas A. Spain, Architect
Pencil on tracing paper 18x24

HOFFPAUIR/ ROSNER STUDIO
Galveston Mardi Gras, Texas (facing page)
Hoffpauir/Rosner Studio, Architects
Watercolor 30x24

PETER A.G. ROPER
Addition to Accord Museum, Montreal
LeMoyne, Lapointe & Magne, Architects
Prismacolor pencil on diazo paper 18x24

CHRISTOPHER GRUBBS
1035-1045 Vallejo Street, San Francisco (above)
Robert A.M. Stern, Architect
Prismacolor on paper 10x16

PETER A.G. ROPER
City Hall Competition, Ottawa (right)
Griffiths, Rankin & Cook, Architects
Prismacolor pencil on mylar 8x8

THOMAS DOLLE*
Redesign of Prudential Tower, Boston (facing page)
Jung/Brannen & Associates, Architects
Colored pencil on mylar 34x80

WILLIAM W. MOORHEAD*
Park Avenue Penthouse, New York (right)
William W. Moorhead, Architect
Oil on canvas 28x44

DONALD C. PAINE
Project for a Gallery, London (below)
Donald Paine, Architect
Airbrush gouache 16x20

MIGUELANGEL GUTIERREZ
Commercial Center (above)
Miguelangel Gutierrez, Architect
Acrylics, airbrush 30x40

EUGENE RADVENIS
Hong Kong Expo '97 (left)
Bing Thom, Architect
Airbrush, marker, pencil 30x30

GORDON GRICE
Governer's Hill, Toronto (facing page)
Rafael Burka, Architect
Ink and pencil on mylar 24x17

ROBERT COOK
Britannia Home, British West Indies
Apex Associates, Architects
Tempera 18x24

FRANK M. COSTANTINO
Becton Dickinson, Franklin Lakes, NJ (above)
Kallmann, McKinnell & Wood, Architects
Pencil on Strathmore 14x27

RICHARD GARDNER
Executive Quarters, Delaware North Company (right)
Joan Hilliers & Company, Architects
Mixed media 28x25

MICHAEL McCANN
University of Southern California at Irvine (above)
Stirling, Wilford Associates, Architects
Watercolor 11x22

SAMUEL RINGMAN*
S&A Headquarters, Dallas (left)
Cunningham Architects
Watercolor 12x12

MARK O'BRYAN*
Monument for the 21st Century (facing page)
Mark O'Bryan, Architect
Mixed media 14x8

RICHARD SNEARY
Mid-American Dairymen, Springfield, MO (left)
Shaugnessey, Fickle & Scott, Architects
Watercolor on art sepia 29x30

SHU-XIANG XI
73 Tremont Street, Boston (below)
Childs, Bertman Tseckares & Casendino, Architects
Watercolor 30x30

RICHARD SNEARY
Pickler Library AdditionKirksville, MO (facing page)
Ittner & Bowersox, Architects
Watercolor on photomural 14x8

LINDA L. MACK*
Mentz Residence
Rebecca Mentz, Architect
Ink tracing paper 20x15

RALPH E. JOHNSON, AIA
Orland Park Village Center (above)
Perkins & Will, Architects
Colored pencil 26x51

LINDA L. MACK
Offices for KBJ Architects, Jacksonvilee, FL (right)
KBJ Architects
Pencil on Letramax board 9x12

EAST—WEST SECTION

ANTHONY ATKIN, AIA
Renfrew Center (above)
Atkin, Voith & Associates, Architects
Watercolor and pencil 30x78

ANTHONY ATKIN, AIA
Derby's Wheel Pump Inn (left)
Anthony Atkin, Architects
Watercolor and pencil 16x20

JEFFREY GEORGE
Community Center, Boston
Kohn, Pedersen Fox, Architects
Graphite, colored pencil 22x30

ANTHONY AMES, FAIA
House at Seaside (left)
Anthony Ames FAIA, Architects
Plastic film on photographic 24x24

ROBERT McALLEN
Ace Market, Los Angeles, CA (below)
Steven Ehrlich, Architect
Acrylic with airbrush 20x30

LEE DUNNETTE, AIA
Greely Block, New York (facing page)
Lee Dunnette, AIA, Architect
Acrylic 40x30

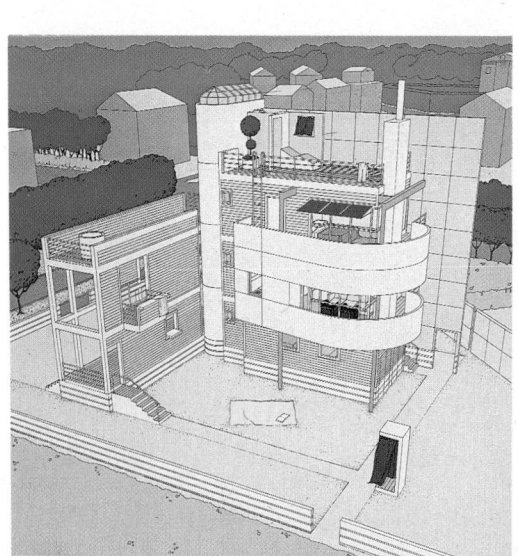

GRIFFIN BLOCK

THE STUDIO OF JAMES C. SMITH
101 North Wacker Drive, Chicago
Anthony Belluschi, Architect
Airbrush 22x45

Architecture In Perspective

V

Introduction

Frank Costantino

For its fifth annual exhibition and convention activities, it was fitting that ASAP elected to come "home" to Boston. Architecture in Perspective V premiered on 14 November 1990 at the World Trade Center as an integral part of Build Boston, the annual convention of the Boston Society of Architects. The BSA, itself a staunch supporter, is a regional chapter of one of ASAP's most powerful and enduring friends, The American Institute of Architects. The Boston venue served to focus the degree of growth and change that ASAP had sustained in the few short years since Architecture In Perspective was last staged there. A far-flung schedule of secondary venues included San Jose, California, Reno, Nevada, the AIA Convention in Washington D.C., Vancouver, Canada and Chicago, lengthening the Society's list of impressive exhibition locations.

The distinguished panel of professionals selected as jurors perhaps had the most faceted experience in design practice, architectural illustration and academia. Robert Campbell AIA, architect and design critic for *The Boston Globe*, Beaux-Arts-trained Jean-Paul Carlhian, FAIA, principal partner in the venerable Boston architectural firm of Shepley Bulfinch Richardson and Abbott, and Lebbeus Woods, architect, illustrator, visiting professor of architecture at Cooper Union and Director of the Research Institute of Experimental Architecture in New York, admirably executed their individual and collective duties. The jury, which convened in Boston in June, was charged with the selection of approximately fifty pieces from a field of three hundred seventy-nine submittals. The implications of their directive soon became readily apparent, for in the words of juror Carlhian, "The overall…quality of the submissions was of the highest level. Here was an array of presentations indicating a mastery of the technique of architectural perspectivism."

Given his insight as a highly regarded illustrator and visionary artist, jury chairman Woods commented on architectural artwork in general, "Good renderings are good not simply because a renderer has illustrating skills, but because drawings present an anticipated world that—like the present one—is all of a piece. Within the anticipated world of the rendering, affinities and disparities emerge with the same clarity as any reality. It is not the renderer's task to prejudice architectural designs, but to construct an aesthetic reality in which judgment as a prelude to action becomes critical." In a comparable assessment, juror Carlhian affirmed "...that the principal mission of the delineator was to represent the subject...at hand with as much fidelity as expected by his client; it is indeed satisfying to witness how well such a task was carried out by members of the Society".

On the specific jury process, Woods observed, "Each member brought his unique point of view and criteria to the judging, but all were concerned with ideas as well as illustrating skills; ideas about architecture, space, form, time and landscape embodied in the submitted renderings. Jury members were often in agreement about renderings lacking strongly coherent concepts, and these were quickly put aside. Agreement was not so easy, however, concerning the stronger renderings, and much of the day was spent in debating the relative merits of a narrowing field of competitors for inclusion in the planned exhibition and an even narrower field for the awards in each category."

The long day was concluded, however, with their selection of exhibit works, three Juror Awards, and unanimous agreement as to the

Category "A" and "B" winners as well as the 1990 Hugh Ferriss Memorial Prize winner, Gilbert Gorski of Chicago. Jury chair Woods, poetically expressing the opinion of the jury, stated: "At their best, rendered architectural perspectives are highly analytical images that anticipate aspects of form, space and time inherent in architectural designs. Yet they also present particular designs as part of the landscape of a world, animated by light common to all things, bound and bracketed by ubiquitous time; a world suffused with particular artistic sensibilities, synthesized by unique artistic vision. I congratulate...ASAP for the maintenance of its high goals and standards, for these alone will nurture and sustain the vital art of architectural illustration." The circumstance and pleasure of the presentation of all awards were highlighted at a properly Bostonian banquet and ceremony following the November show opening.

ARCHITECTURE IN PERSPECTIVE V 1990
Jurors Campbell, Woods, and Carlhian (facing page)

The Hugh Ferriss Memorial Prize

The recipient of the 1990 Hugh Ferriss Memorial Prize is Gilbert Gorski, AIA, for his masterful work, "The Interior of the Basilica Ulpia; Trajan's Forum, Rome." The Chicago-based architect/artist completed the work as one in a series of commissioned pieces for an archaeological study based upon the reconstruction of monuments of the Forum of Trajan in ancient Rome. This particular piece depicts the interior of the Basilica Ulpia, one of the major edifices of the Forum, as it most probably appeared in the second century A.D.

"This is more than mere representation." So stated juror Carlhian, who went on to cite Mr. Gorski's "…choice of vanishing point [as] most felicitious, the resulting drawing dividing the space into harmonious proportions. Most effective was the handling of light, conveying a wonderful sense of grandeur and mystery at the same time. The result proved most evocative and therefore appropriate to the importance of a subject matter of such historical implication."

Juror Woods on Mr. Gorski's winning entry added: "It presents us with a potent and animate world that can be entered with full faculties. The space engages the mind as well as the eye, because the rendering of light reveals not only the physical nature of the architecture, but also the connection of this place with a wider world beyond. The drawing embodies a particular moment of a world to the degree that one may enter into its place

completely. The originality of the drawing lies in its point of view, mysteriously high and to the left of the space—a distinctly modern bit of abstraction in placement of the viewer. It does not ape the older, historicist drawings of similar subjects, but instead gives the viewer a highly individual, privileged glimpse of a vanished, but still vivid, ancient world."

The realism of the ceiling, the accuracy of the colonnade and its shadow, the effusiveness of a bright Roman sky and the cool, shaded interior of a majestic place are remarkably illustrated in a rich palette of color pencils. Indeed, the timeless impact of "Basilica Ulpia," a major factor justifying its distinction as the Ferriss Prize winner, has, through the power of Mr. Gorski's time-removed depiction, effected a chronological link with his twentieth century interpretation of second century architecture.

GILBERT GORSKI, AIA
The Interior of the Basilica Ulpia; Trajan's Forum, Rome
Professor James Packer, Northwestern University
Harry Weese and Associates, Architects
Pencil and airbrush on illustration board 19x26

Category "A" Award

FRANK M. COSTANTINO
Chicago Public Library Competition
Hammond, Beeby & Babka, Architects
Graphite pencil on vellum 11x16

Frank M. Costantino was the unanimous jury choice for "Best in Category 'A'—Formal Presentation Drawings" for his imposing pencil rendition of the proposed facade of the Harold Washington Library in Chicago. One of a number of design competition drawings, the work was executed on vellum and was planned with a deliberately close viewing angle to accentuate the monumentality of the facade, feature the exuberant Beaux-Arts detailing, and emphasize the library's formal presence at street level.

This was, to quote juror Woods, "a classic rendering of a classical architectural design. What most struck the jurors was the palpable presence in the drawing of sunlight seeming to carve the architecture with the force of its precision and clarity, presenting an architecture of lightness and gravity at once…"

"The decision," observed juror Carlhian, "to represent only a part of the building and the resulting closeness of the facade to the viewer conveyed the importance of this structure as a monument of the city. By filling the page, it enticed the viewer to imagine what was missing. A grand rendering."

Category "B" Award

"Da Vinci Detail," a watercolor of a design for a commissioned wall mural, by artist/designer Martin Myers of Toronto, was selected as "Best in Category 'B'—Sketches and Conceptual Drawings." The drawing represents only a small portion of the extensive mural (4x20 feet, consisting of sixteen detail panels in watercolor) designed for a Toronto architect's office. "A rich and engaging story beautifully told," summarized juror Carlhian of Mr. Myer's fanciful work. He continued, "A wonderful evocation of Leonardo's genius. The choice of vignetting in this case was most appropriate in suggesting the range of DaVinci's interests. The composition articulated around the campanile divided the sheet harmoniously, bringing the right kind of repose in the right place of a composition…"

"A deftly rendered arabesque" was juror Woods descriptive phrase for Myer's piece, "selected as much for its ingenious conceptual interweavings as for its skillfulness as illustration."

MARTIN MYERS*
DaVinci Detail, design for a commissioned mural
Bregman & Hamann, Architects
Watercolor 22x30

Juror Award

DOUGLAS E. JAMIESON
Library Tower, Los Angeles
Pei, Cobb, Freed & Partners, Architects
India ink, airbrush and wash 39x29

"Library Tower," an ink-wash and airbrush drawing of a high-rise proposal for Los Angeles, earned a 1990 Architecture in Perspective V Juror Award for Douglas E. Jamieson of Pacific Palisades, California. Jamieson's all black-and-white work, characterized by an uncommon strength of composition and execution, highly impressed the Beaux-Arts-trained juror Jean-Paul Carlhian.

"The jury was presented with a great number of high-rise building submissions," wrote Mr. Carlhian, "most of these were precisely indicated and punctiliously drawn—achieving, therefore, a perfect representation of the subject at hand."

"In this case, however," juror Carlhian continued, "the author managed to evoke the sublime grandeur of man's aspiration in trying to reach the sky. This was accomplished by the decision to backlight the subject while throwing one of its faces in a blinding light reaching to its very top." Though surely different in approach and technique, there is a quality in Jamieson's piece which is distinctly reminiscent of the work of Hugh Ferriss. The choice of subject matter—the high-rise structure—is the most important (though only one) of the many elements in an overall composition. Shade and shadow are boldly sculpted and confidently orchestrated to dramatic chiaroscuro effect.

Of his juror selection, Mr. Carlhian concluded: "Accompanying low structures, kept dark in value, pursue the lighting theme down to the ground with great finesse. We need not actually see how the building hits the ground. No distracting cars and people are called for. All that counts is the soaring dark value of the building silhouetted against a light sky growing dark as the building rises and catches the raking light at its apex. This is a true evocation, in the grand manner, of the architect's soaring aspiration."

Juror Award

Describing his selected entry for a 1990 Juror's Award, "One Detroit Center" by the Houston, Texas-based architectural illustration team Stephan Hoffpauir and Joyce Rosner, juror Robert Campbell wrote, "By floating three enigmatic symbols above a view of an interior, the renderer reminds us of some of the central issues of architecture: the relation between enclosure and the beyond, the framing and measuring of volume and proportion. The symbols are a commentary on the space beneath them, which is rendered with great skill. The whole is an unforgettable image that fuses the real with the ideal."

Hoffpauir/Rosner elaborated on the premise for this piece: "What struck us most about this space was the sense of its being made up of repeating frames. Besides the pattern of small stone frames in the walls, there are the frames of the doors, the windows, the floor pattern, and the ceiling. Even the rectangular floor plan of this lobby seemed to be based on some predetermined frame proportion. The 'unit of measurement,' so to speak, of this spatial composition appeared to be the repeating red, yellow, and black stone panels which make up the wall pattern. The preciousness of the rather exotically colored stones is alluded to in the ornate gilded frame in the upper center of the drawing. The gilded frame, like the space itself, is empty, a spectacular void where the emphasis is what surrounds and not on what is surrounded. In the drawing's upper left hand corner is the 'painting' meant to be in the frame. The egg, made of white stone blocks, floats in the sky, its lightness belying its mass and weight. It is intended to evoke feelings related to birth, death, and immortality. The red line proportional diagram on the right explains the geometric relationship of the painting to the wall panels and how the composition of the painting was derived. The diagram is an allusion to those which often appear in architectural history books where diagrams are used to show the facade proportions of buildings."

HOFFPAUIR/ROSNER STUDIO
One Detroit Center, Detroit
John Burgee, Architects
Watercolor 28x38

Juror Award

Jury chair Lebbeus Woods: "My selection [for 1990 Juror Award] was Michael Reardon's rooftop vista of a city at night. It is a masterful rendering of a total landscape that reaches from the intimate presence of architecture and human activity in the foreground to the threshold of the cosmos, lying beyond the horizon and the dimly silhouetted clouds through which intense moonlight is breaking. Between these extremes lies a city, its presence on the surface of earth exposed as a rational grid of light. This is a depicted world of light, not at its reflected surface, but at its multiple sources. Nature and man are presented equally as radiant sources, entities of light energies permeating and sharing a landscape of cosmic proportions. This rendering is bold and risky in its execution…a tour de force…it lies at the boundary of the visionary."

MICHAEL REARDON
Capitol Mall Competition, Sacramento, CA
Skidmore, Owings & Merrill, Architects
Charcoal and pencil on Mylar 15x19

Selected Entries

HOFFPAUIR/ROSNER STUDIO*
Still Life with Architectural Models
Pencil on paper 22x22

MICHAEL REARDON
39 Stockton Street, San Francisco
Silver & Ziskind, Architects
Pencil on mylar 20x16

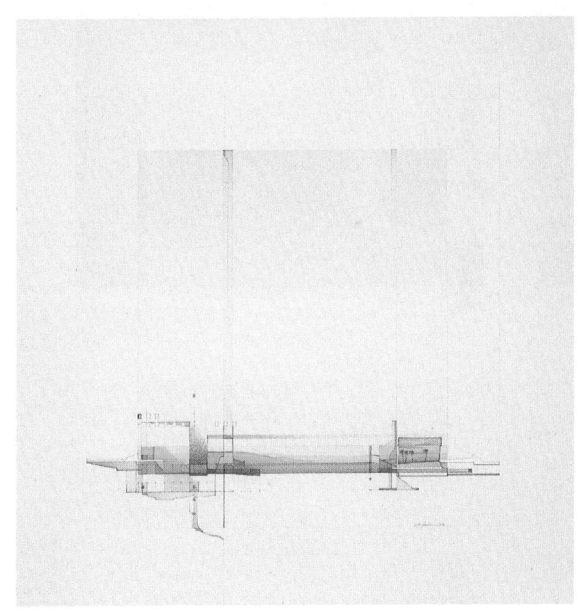

BRENT A. MAUGEL, AIA
Chinatown Community Facility, Boston (above)
Donnelly Maugel, Architects
Ink on mylar 12x21

RICHARD B. FERRIER, AIA*
Horizontal Condition: Edge of the Painted Landscape (right)
Richard B. Ferrier, AIA, Architect
Mixed media 22x22

WILLIAM WILDE
150 Post Street Renovation, San Francisco (above)
Gensler & Associates, Architects
Prismacolor paper 24x36

PETER HUF
Brewster (left)
A. Anthony Tappe & Associates, Architects
Computer image 17x24

PHILIPPE MARTYNIAK
Case Western Reserve University, Cleveland (facing page)
Payette Associates, Architects
Pastel and pencil paper 40x30

LEE DUNNETTE, AIA
Subway Kiosk at Bowling Green Station, New York (above)
Weintraub, diDomenico & Massand, Architects
Freehand ink and airbrush 13x18

LEE DUNNETTE, AIA*
Astronaut's Memorial (E.T.) (left)
Lee Dunnette, AIA, Architect
Pastel 25x25

RONALD J. LOVE
City Gate, Phase II, Vancouver
Perkins & Cheung, Architects
Pen and ink and acrylic 23x23

OREST ASSOCIATES
South Ferry Plaza, New York City (facing page)
Arquitectonica, Architects
Tempera 40x30

RICHARD BERGMANN, FAIA*
Life Span Continuing Care Facility (right)
Richard Bergmann Architects
Fiber tip pen 15x24

MICHAEL ELAVSKY
Madison Square Garden, New York City (below)
Ellerbe & Becket, Architects
Marker, pencil paper 15x24

GILBERT GORSKI, AIA*
Demeter and Dionysus (facing page)
Gilbert Gorski, AIA, Architect
Color pencil 15x10

RICHARD LOVELACE
Residential Towers, Massing Sketch, New York City (right)
Beyer, Blinder, Belle, Architects
Charcoal pencil on paper 7x7

JAMES FOX
Grand Central Station, New York City (below)
Beyer, Blinder & Belle/Harry Weese, Archiitects
Prismacolor on mylar 19x32

CHRISTOPHER GRUBBS*
Hotel Quint, Okinawa (above)
Projects International, Architects
Prismacolor 10x15

CHRISTOPHER GRUBBS
Marina Linear Park, San Diego (left)
Peter Walker & Partners, Architects
Prismacolor 16x26

DOUGLAS E. JAMIESON
Grand Place, Los Angeles (facing page)
Skidmore, Owings & Merrill, Architects
Mixed media 39x29

PAUL STEVENSON OLES, FAIA
Canary Wharf, London (facing page)
Cesar Pelli & Associates, Architects
Prismacolor on black illustration board 18x13

GEORGE T. GINTOLE*
Domestic Quadrangles (right)
George T. Gintole, Architect
Mixed media 32x34

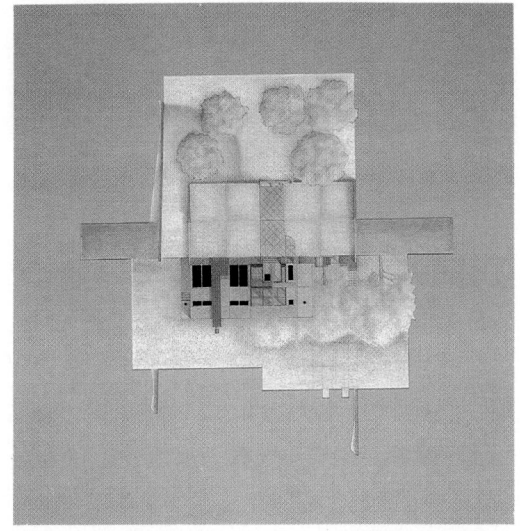

PAUL STEVENSON OLES, FAIA
Canary Wharf, London (below)
Cesar Pelli & Associates, Architects
Prismacolor on black illustration board 12x19

PETER A. G. ROPER
Proposed Lighting, Imperial War Museum, Ottawa (above)
Gabriel Design, Architects
Prismacolor on diazo paper 7x23

WILLIAM G. HOOK*
Study Sketch, Stevens School Renovation, Seattle (left)
Pencil on paper 11x9

PETER A.G. ROPER
New Galleria, Grand Central Station, New York (facing page)
Beyer, Blinder & Belle/Harry Weese & Associates
Prismacolor on mylar 27x23

EUGENE V. RADVENIS
Canada Pavilion, Expo '92, Sevilla, Spain
Bing Thom Architects
Mixed media 20x20

THE STUDIO OF JAMES C. SMITH
Meridian Business Campus, Fort Lauderdale (above)
Richard A.M. Potokar, Architect
Airbrushed polymer 25x44

TANIER ASSOCIATES
Villa Quadrata, Prospect Heights, IL (right)
Tanier Associates, Architects
Airbrush, marker and paint 26x26

FRANK M. COSTANTINO
Hynes Memorial Auditorium, Boston (above)
Kallmann, McKinnell & Wood, Architects
Prismacolor on mylar 30x36

JEFFERY S. POSS
Tribute to Olympic Athletes, Champaign Park, IL (left)
Jeffrey S. Poss/ Isaken Matzdorf & Associates, Architect
Brushed ink with pastel 17x29

DAN HARMON
Moscow Center, Moscow (facing page)
John Portman & Associates, Architects
Watercolor 32x22

THOMAS W. SCHALLER
U.S. Courthouse, New York City (facing page)
Kohn, Pedersen, Fox & Associates, Architects
Watercolor 40x30

THOMAS W. SCHALLER
Federal Triangle, Washington, DC (right)
Kohn, Pedersen, Fox & Associates, Architects
Watercolor 24x24

BARBARA WORTH RATNER*
The Wave, Fort Lauderdale (below)
Cooper, Carry & Associates, Architects
Colored overlay film 5x13

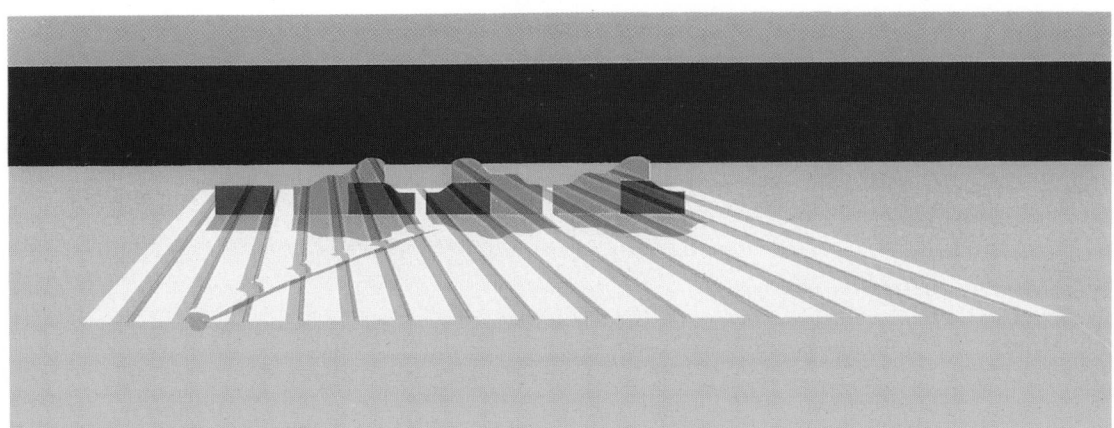

RICHARD SNEARY
Hill's Project Quest, Richmond, IN (right)
A. Epstein & Sons, Architects
Watercolor 14x25

BILL ROSS
The Alberta Temple, Cardston, Canada (below)
Gowling & Gibb, Architects
Watercolor 24x39

ROBERT McILHARGEY
Entertainment Complex (facing page)
Waisman, Dewar, Grout, Carter, Architects
Mixed media 48x36

STANLEY DOCTOR
International Airport, Denver (above)
Perez Architects
Prismacolor and gouache 26x40

DONGIK LEE
Palm Restaurant at Cocoa, Orlando (left)
Graham Gund Associates, Architects
Watercolor 24x36

JAMES B. McBURNEY
New Ukranian Orthodox Church, Arden Hills, MN
Frank D. Nemeth, Architect
Watercolor, pencil and ink 19x21

WEST ELEVATION

ELIZABETH ANN DAY
U.S. Courthouse Competition, New York City (facing page)
Kohn, Pedersen & Fox Associates, Architects
Watercolor 40x30

ELIZABETH ANN DAY
U.S. Courthouse Competition, New York City (right)
Kohn, Pedersen & Fox Associates, Architects
Watercolor 40x30

JEFFREY MICHAEL GEORGE
La Bahia, Santa Cruz, CA (below)
Daniel Mann Johnson Mendenhall, Architects
Pencil 13x45

SAMUEL C. RINGMAN
Cliff House (above)
Guerin Architecture, Architects
Watercolor and pencil 10x20

DAVID DAWSON
Gateway to Muskoka Lakes, Ontario, Canada (left)
Town of Gravenhurst, Architects
Tempera 12x18

SHU-XIANG XI
Smithsonian Institution, Washington, DC (facing page)
Shepley, Bulfinch, Richardson & Abbott, Architects
Ink brush 23x18

Artists' Directory and Commentary

Anthony Ames
House at Seaside (IV), page 154

Marshall (Andy) Anderson
One Kansas City Place (I), page 24

Chris Anderson
Proposal for an Idaho Farmhouse (IV), page 119
(Category "B" Award, 1989)

Anthony Atkin
Derby's Wheel Pump Inn (IV), page 152
Renfrew Center (IV), page 152

Susan Austin-Salvo
Lake Center Executive Park (I), page 34

Richard C. Baehr, AIA
International Place (I), page 19
The painting's challenge was to clearly define all the elements of this complex design; the perspective required 23 vanishing points. The sun angle utilized direct light, glancing light, shade, and shadow to fully emphasize the relationships of the volumes.

Williamsburg Bridge (III), page 106

Frank Bartus
University of South Florida (III), page 108

Richard Bergmann, FAIA
St. Michael's Lutheran Church (III), page 97
The drawing was a composite of both positive and negative pen-and-ink drawings. The composite was then photostated into its final form with red numbers (dates) for accent color.

Life Span Continuing Care Facility (V), page 175
To quickly depict conceptual views, a two-hour technique for this piece was multi-duplicating a segment of leaf texture onto clear acetate sheets and "pasting up" the foreground foliage. The tree trunks were cut out and the whole copied. The joints and overlaps were then "fixed up." The buildings were sketched in and silhouetted with felt-tip-pen-drawn background foliage.

Robert J. Berry
Holiday Inn (I), page 25
Derived from photos, visits, and drawings of the abandoned granite quarry site, the delineation expresses the structure integrated to the site and not intrusive upon it. Pen and ink was the appropriate medium to portray the rugged beauty of the area.

John Blood
Museum of Ansel Adams Photographs (III), page 110

Bruce Bondy
Galati Tower (IV), page 134
This pen and ink drawing was part of an exhibition titled "Experimental Skytowers," an opportunity for architects to explore high-rise construction concepts, free from budget limitations and technical requirements. Located on an island in Lake Michigan, this tower rises above the treetops. While the Galati Tower was drawn as designed, the landscape evokes an atmosphere of repose, a place for thoughtfulness.

Sarah Brannen
Winter Garden, Beal Office Building (IV), page 123
This rendering was most successful for the architects; the client detested it, finding it "threatening."

Mona Brown
The Bromley (I), page 38
City Hall Competition (II), page 78
Supreme Court Competition (II), page 80
Convention Center (IV), page 132

Ernest Burden III
Faison Building (II), page 77

Brent Byers, FAIA
The Ozark Building Lobby (I), page 41
This drawing illustrated a remodeling in an existing 1920s structure. Clarity and simplicity helped communicate the singular idea of materials usage and design in enhancing the marble staircase.

Old City Jail (II), page 72
A simple representation of the structure's final renovation, the drawing accurately depicts the building's reconstruction and its compatibility with the surrounding historic district. The media convey a sense of cleanliness, realism, and simplicity.

Dallas Ballet (II), page 73

Robert Comazzi
Exeter Street Theater (II), page 67
A Beaux-Arts-style watercolor was an appropriate and powerful way to represent the fanciful forms and details of this historic Boston building. An elevation served as a base drawing. The richly ornamented facade was carefully recorded on site through sketches and notations. The illustration also proved useful as a historical record.

Robert Cook
Cliff House (I), page 20
This rendering was a self-advertising painting to show the studio's vignette technique using as many rendering elements as possible, i.e.: mountains, pastel clouds, rocks, cars, and trees were planned into the piece.

McKinney/Monticello Office (II), page 66
Poydras Square Shopping Center (II), page 66
The complex curves and angles of the large vaulted skylight were computer-generated. All materials were realistically depicted.

Britannia Home (IV), page 144
This interior conveys the soft pastel colors typical of the islands (with a view across the golf course).

Frank M. Costantino

176 Federal Street (II), page 52
Although all but the new penthouse floor existed, the perspective was projected from drawings rather than traced from photographs. The raking light and steep shadows on the foreshortened facade, together with the slightly stronger value contrast on the subject building, established an effective presence in both drawing and architecture. Assisted by Arthur Dutton and Catherine Blank.

Peabody Museum (II), page 53
Since this tightly sited Asian Wing of an existing museum presented only one access, the constraining options for viewpoints proved to be an asset in the drawing's composition. The strong geometry and varied materials of a northerly elevation demanded a delicate handling of surfaces in shade. A contrast reversal between light and shadow accented the dynamics of layered entourage and depth of space. The extended tonal range depicting a bright atmosphere and deep shadows create the tranquil mood of a secluded oriental garden enclosed by the wing's moon-gate wall. Assisted by Arthur Dutton.

Becton Dickinson (II), page 53
This wide view, showing the more interesting projecting "fingers" of the rear facade, is punctuated by the trees of a densely wooded site. The architect increased the hesitant illustrator's original number of trees, creating a difficult compositional problem of carefully layering trunks, branches, and leaves over the architecture. The seductive atmosphere of evening enhanced the play of light between the exterior and interior, and the autumnal foliage effected the undisturbed nature of the grounds. Color-pencil was applied to both front and back of a mylar photo of the original black-and-white image. Assisted by Arthur Dutton.

Main Aquarium Tank (III), page 110
Floundering with an unfamiliar subject, the poetic vision of an architect, an unforgiving schedule, and the most uncorrectable of media, the artist's solution derived more from the process of painting than any intent of representation. The numerous washes of blues created the translucent watery depths of the aquarium's sunlit surface. The exhibit designer's input on species and habit of fish allowed for an effective composition of sea life. Photos from the architect were the perfect reference for the Japanese children. Assisted by Arthur Dutton.

Pier Four (III), page 111
The gangly proportions of a tall, narrow, long atrium space was balanced by the steeply projected shadow of this view. The coarse, vigorous pencil strokes, a technique effected as much by the tight schedule and numerous design changes as by the texture of the toothy drawing paper, resulted in the "sketchy" quality of a field drawing at a completed atrium. Assisted by Arthur Dutton and Catherine Blank.

Becton Dickinson (IV), page 145
The lengthy dimensions of a winged design, a complex gradient with its roadway, and the contrast of a manicured landscape with an existing wooded site required a studied juxtaposition of these elements into the composition. The building's scale was intentionally diminished by the extended sky area, which also provided the balance of space to the emphatic horizontality of the architecture and road. Similarly, the few vertical accents of trees establish the depth of field and play of light that enhanced the architect's skillful siting. The high-resolution pencil work was drawn on a medium-surface strathmore paper. Assisted by Arthur Dutton and Catherine Costantino.

Chicago Public Library Competition (V), page 162
(Category "A" Award, 1990)

Hynes Memorial Auditorium (V), page 186
With a slightly elevated horizon to better describe the plaza areas, the slender end of the building became the principal focus, contrasting sharply with a very foreshortened, colonnaded facade punctuated by the projecting entrance canopy. As important counterbalancing elements to the convergence, the dramatic roof side shadows were developed. Together with the major street shadow, a studied cloud configuration, and a sliver of an adjacent building, the major angles of the composition were carefully juxtaposed for a dynamic but balanced effect. Assisted by Arthur Dutton.

Terry A. Cracknell
James Landing (I), page 42
Residence (III), page 96

Mark Patin Crow
Residential Interior (IV), page 133

David Dawson
Gateway to Muskoka Lakes (V), page 196
The Gravenhurst Gateway is the last of a few restored public structures in the tourist town of Gravenhurst, Ontario. The archway speaks to a time of optimism and plenty, the 1920s, when the tourist was king and "motoring out" on gravel roads was fun. The archway marked the start of a holiday or a return to home. It was a punctuation mark on the famous Ferguson Highway from Toronto to the north.

Elizabeth Ann Day

The Wellington (I), page 40
Mellon Bank (II), page 48
Mellon Bank, Interior Perspective, Concourse (III), page 109

U.S. Courthouse, West Elevation (V), page 194
U.S. Courthouse, South Elevation (V), page 195
Representing sculptural form and creating a realistic presence in an elevation drawing can be an absorbing problem. The range of visual cues is limited, which, for the illustrator, reduces some decision-making, but requires close attention to the handling of value, shadow, and color to describe the undelineated plane changes, curves, transparency, reflectance, and texture.

Ed DeLara

Park Central Development (I), page 36
This piece was an innovative utilization of colored markers. The ink linework was done on vellum, then photoprinted on clear acetate. Serving as underlay, a high-grade tracing paper was used, on which color was applied. The artwork was then laminated together on a stiff board and mounted. The result was a crisp drawing with photo-realistic qualities.

Carlos Diniz

Canary Wharf (III), page 96

Stanley Doctor

Colorado Gateway Convention Center (II), page 70
The drawing was prepared for a last-minute bid on a new downtown Convention Center. Included in the concept rendition was the development of the valley, complete with rapid-transit system, new baseball stadium, residences and offices, riverfront improvements, and amusement park. A night view was chosen both for its dramatic effect and the extremely conceptual nature of the design.

Townhouses at Beaver Creek (IV), page 125
To describe a series of condominiums in an exclusive Colorado ski resort, the most important goal of the drawing was to convey a sense of the place, with the aspens, the skiers, the snow. Secondly, a wintry mood was suggested with soft lighting, light cloudy sky, and thick falling snow. The result was a romantic drawing with a sophisticated corniness that worked very well.

Denver International Airport (V), page 192
The architect required a single drawing depicting all functions of the building. Because of the various levels and spaces, a section perspective was the obvious choice. A night drawing emphasized the main interior and allowed the hypothetical view to float in space to avoid confusion with any context. Conceptual design level drawings were used to input the computer drawing system. Values and entourage were hand-drawn directly on the plot, which was then printed on blackline paper, mounted, and colored with a variety of wet and dry media.

Thomas Dolle, AIA

Redesign of Prudential Tower (IV), page 140

Lee Dunnette, AIA

Worth Square Building (I), page 15
(Best of Show, 1986)

Teddy Chair (III), page 86
"Teddy Chair" is an unusual example of using the "users'" viewpoint (toddlers play on their tummies).

Two Times Square (III), page 87
Clients commission renderings for practical purposes, and renderers are paid to satisfy those requirements. "Two Times Square" happens to satisfy a rigorous function (selling sign space), while portraying the intangible essence of Times Square.

Greely Block (IV), page 155

Subway Kiosk at Bowling Green Station (V), page 172
A surprisingly evocative view of an urban scene, considering that it was produced at a secluded mountain cabin. A night version was also produced from this drawing.

Astronaut's Memorial (E.T.) (V), page 172
An experiment in an unfamiliar medium, proving that pastel has high potential in architectural rendering, and that the artist won't be the one to fulfill that potential.

James Earl

Riverbend Office Park (I), page 30

Michael Elavsky

University of Notre Dame (III), page 88
ConAgra, Corporate Headquarters (III), page 89

Madison Square Garden (V), page 175
This project was drawn from a photo underlay (devoid of people and activity, however). Given that base, redrawing the space, adding new skybox suites, scoreboard, and end-zone seating, then peopling it convincingly, was a gargantuan task nonetheless. The real challenge was drawing a convincing mass of people. Showing interaction among the foreground figures made them convincing as human beings and set the mood for the arena environment. The viewer's imagination animates the distant masses.

Wendy Evans, AIA

Architectural Fantasy (I), page 18
This study was done while a Fellow in Architecture at the American Academy in Rome. It uses both traditional perspectival methods as well as pre-Rennaissance techniques of overlapping images. Multiple readings are possible due to a complex series of vanishing points.

Holocaust Memorial Museum (II), page 78
This early sketch for a client presentation was drawn to evoke the feeling of mass and light rather than to portray the actual details of construction.

Stephan S. Evanusa, AIA

Syrigos Residence (I), page 31
Bryan Residence (II), page 74
Adirondack Residence (II), page 75

Richard B. Ferrier, AIA

Bevoni Residence (I), page 16
My clients allowed a level of communication and interaction that was both conceptual as well as pragmatic. The composite drawing illustrated the relationship of plan, elevation, and site considerations. The perspective sketches depicted literal notions of the built forms and site development. The intention was similar to drawings from the Beaux-Arts: that the juxtaposition of the component parts might reveal inherent relationships which would exceed one's comprehension based on independent representations of plan, elevation, site, and perspective.

"Windows and Fragments": Narrative Visions (IV), page 126
For several years the "Windows and Fragments" drawing series was an investigation of architectural ideas. "Narrative Visions" consists of a broad array of images including architectural projects, objects by Karl Friedrich Schinkel, landscapes, windows with photographic film transparencies, metal construction, collage, and applied "dollhouse" wallpaper tinted with color pencil and graphite. Cuts in the surface, washes, and articulated surfaces contribute to this drawing. With this drawing type, discovery is more significant than architectural or literal depictions.

The Horizontal Condition:
Edge of the Painted Landscape (V), page 169
This drawing is based on conceptual notions which investigate the relationships of architectural fragments and the horizontal condition. This condition evokes a human response to define the realm of proper dimension and the nature of structures juxtaposed within the vast nature of horizon and sky. Layers of perceived space and planes are likely participants. These perceptions can be real, conceptual, and/or metaphoric. It is the very nature of perception that new attitudes and conditions allow alternative visions of these design determinants.

Brian Fisher and Rich Poling

Hibiscus House (II), page 74
"Hibiscus House" was a gouache rendition in a multiple-view composition to best consolidate the project's design information. The gouache was applied by brush as a base coat, and then airbrush, as a final coat, covered the brush-strokes to effect a silkscreened look. This effect creates an overall surrealistic impression. By using minimal entourage and high contrast between the architectural elements in the foreground and the sky as background, the surrealistic mood is also enhanced by a late afternoon lighting casting long shadows across the perspective.

James Fox

Grand Central Station (V), page 177
Peter Roper and I developed a technique for pencil work with which the presentation of eleven sections and perspectives would be unified, as each of us were to complete drawings individually.

Robert Frank

Cinema 7 (II), page 64
This carbon pencil drawing is a strong personal expression of evocative visual images. Made up of powerful, individual marks, they create a drawing that conveys the mystique of night. The ambiguity in the architectural details refers to the heightened lit night.

Richard Gardner

Executive Quarters, Delaware North Company (IV), page 145

James Garland

Johnson Residence (III), page 112

Jeffrey Michael George

101 Federal Street (I), page 32
The challenge of this interior rendering was depicting the character of the stone. The use of a pencil with a broad, flat chisel point yielded a similar effect to the subtle veining of the selected marble.

Community Center (IV), page 153
The key technique of this drawing was the consistent use of a blunt pencil point to create a "unique calligraphy" of architectural detail. A concerted effort was made to avoid drawing lines—but instead, "paint" only shaded surfaces of various sizes, using broad, sometimes very short strokes of the pencil.

La Bahia (V), page 195
This rendering allows the architecture itself to "welcome" the viewer—without the usual distraction of people and cars. The image suggests the viewer taking an early Sunday morning stroll along the boardwalk, before the rest of the world has risen.

George T. Gintole

Domestic Quadrangles (V), page 181
This project was derived from the American campus quadrangle as a unifying field of space. Using the Latin derivation of the word "campus"—meaning "field", the green "lawn" has become a quintessentially American emblem. Not only does it manifest itself as a positive "additive" element in our landscape, but also as a vestige of the former forest floor, or "wilderness," from which our cities are carved. The drawing itself is a direct response to the 1948 essay "Le Doute de Cézanne" (Cézanne's Doubt), where Cézanne's way of organizing a painting was predicated on the struggle to paint the world as it appeared to him. It also verifies the notion that spatial deviations could be as accurate as those ordered according to an a-priori system. The drawing gives the impression of a scheme in the act of appearing, and that an art of personal expression can have a universal sense.

Gilbert Gorski, AIA
Riverwalk for Cityfront Center (II), page 48
181 Madison Building (IV), page 120
(Juror Award, 1989)

The Baths of Schaumburg (IV), page 128
"The Baths of Schaumburg" was created as a submission to the Alternative Visions Exhibition sponsored by the Cultural Center of Chicago in 1989. The exhibition challenged architects to "...submit an architectural idea that responds to an anticipated or unforeseen change in Chicago's condition..." Attached to the drawing at the exhibit was the following statement: "In the not too distant future critical water shortage in outlying suburbs deprived of lake water will force some communities to resort to public bathing as a means to conserve. Consider the Baths of Schaumburg."

Trajan's Forum (V), page 161
(Hugh Ferriss Memorial Prize Winner, 1990)

Demeter & Dionysus (V), page 176
Sensing an incomplete knowledge of their world, the ancient Greeks invented myths to help order their existence. This offering was created anticipating a society more aware of its incomplete knowledge.

Eric Gould
Marshfield Hills (I), page 39

Gordon Grice
Governer's Hill (IV), page 143
Gardens are an ideal subject for pen-and-ink illustration since their representation relies on elaborate textures. Regarding the coloring of the drawing, my client, an engineer, played an unusually large role. He simply refused to accept the drawing until it was the artist's very best. Each time he was shown the "completed" drawing, he pointed to a weakness and asked that it be improved. The success of the drawing owes much to his skill as a good critic.

Christopher Grubbs
Hyatt Fantasy Resort (III), page 100
California State University Competition (III), page 100
1035-1045 Vallejo Street (IV), page 139

Marina Linear Park (V), page 178
A model of the project plus a good camera shot provided a time-saving base for this drawing.

Hotel Quint (V), page 178
A simple perspective of the hotel's mass provided a framework upon which to quickly test competing stylistic schemes. Construction of the perspective was followed by equal time for exploratory studies and the final drawing; the total production time was 14.5 hours.

Michael Guran
The Courtyards (III), page 112

Miguelangel Guttierrez
Restaurant (I), page 41
Dallas Main Center (II), page 55
Commercial Center (IV), page 142

James Hadley
Round Hill Estate (III), page 108

Dan Harmon
400 Peachtree (III), page 104

Moscow Center (V), page 187
Part of a series, this view was chosen for its relationship to a prominent intersection and a recognizable landmark in the distance.

Andrew Hickes
Transpotomac Canal Center (II), page 61

Plaza at Rio Condominiums (II), page 61
The night view of the atrium was achieved with a blue acetate overlay on a large photograph of the daytime rendering. The result is the appearance of two renderings but with minimal extra time.

Hoffpauir/Rosner Studio
LTV Tower (II), page 54
Memphis Brooks Museum of Art (III), page 98
Memphis Brooks Museum of Art (IV), page 136
Galveston Mardi Gras (IV), page 137

One Detroit Center (V), page 165
(Juror Award, 1990)

Still Life with Architectural Models (V), page 167
The drawing was inspired by Sir John Soane's "Public and Private Buildings," a drawing of assembled models of buildings designed by Soane. These white foamcore models (the pyramid and the dome, for example) were selected for their formal, geometric qualities. The models, which were never intended to be seen together, are built at different scales, creating a sense of contradiction and tension in the drawing borne out of the disparity in scales. The drawing is executed with an HB pencil on Rives BFK paper.

Holt Hinshaw Pfau Jones
Warden's House (IV), page 121

William G. Hook
Ingram Stagen Residence (II), page 72
The architectural character of this residence provided the first opportunity to experiment with a traditional Beaux-Arts rendering technique of ink washes and watercolor.

Franklin High School (III), page 106
An unfortunate 1950s classroom addition to the front obliterated the school's scale and classical image. A major public effort resulted in saving the school and restoring its presence. It's hard to miss with such a painting—when the building has character and Olmsted set up the view.

Centrum Performance Center (III), page 106
This conversion of a WWI balloon hangar into a Performing Arts Center was probably the only opportunity to justify a balloon in the sky.

Study Sketch, Stevens School Renovation (V), page 182
It seems that so often a quick composition and value study can capture a quality of light, spirit and energy which is almost impossible to translate into a final presentation... maybe someday.

Peter Huf (with Philippe Martyniak)
Brewster (V), page 170
Sometimes abstract visual ideas can be more compelling than a strict interpretation of a floor plan.

Suns Hung
The Rizzoli Building (II), page 68
Three Park Avenue (II), page 69

Remmert W. Huygens, FAIA
Longy School of Music (I), page 33

Douglas E. Jamieson
Library Tower (V), page 164
(Juror Award, 1990)
Grand Place (V), page 179

Ralph E. Johnson, AIA
Orland Park Village Center (IV), page 151

Don M. Jones, AIA
Bryn Mawr Campus Center (I), page 22

David Mark Lane, AIA
The Base (III), page 92
Pen-and-ink drawing on Mylar provides the client with an original reproducible by diazo printing. The drawing was traced from a slide of the architect's model. Building details and landscape were then added until the final pen-and-ink drawing was completed. To produce this colored version, a brown-line print was painted by marker and colored pencil. The drawing has a watercolor/gouache sky, which had been separately painted on board; the colored print (lower portion) was affixed to it.

Bruce A. Lavalee
Halcyon Limited (I), page 27

Dongik Lee
Austin City Hall (II), page 70
Austin Nature Center (II), page 70
Palm Restaurant at Cocoa (V), page 192

Dean B. Lewis
"The Overlook" (II), page 76

Jonathan Levi
Residence in Boylston (IV), page 118
(Category "A" Award, 1989)

Rolando Llanes
Courtyard study (I), page 16

Ronald J. Love
City Gate, Phase II (V), page 173
To illustrate the condominium tower and its relation to the surrounding towers and foreground park, the tower was featured as the main focal point in the center of the composition. The park with its beautiful large trees set the mood of the picture. The tower was rendered in sharp focus, with more detail and color than the context. To imply the idea of luxury and quality, a soft, subdued color was applied, with linework carrying the drawing. The medium was pen and ink on Strathmore drawing paper. Color was applied using airbrush.

Richard Lovelace
One Montvale Avenue (II), page 47
(Hugh Ferriss Memorial Prize Winner)

Erie Community College (II), page 76
A Winter Garden, Waterfront Competition (III), page 99
The Lagoon, Waterfront Competition (III), page 99
Civic Plaza and Office Towers (IV), page 127

Residential Towers (V), page 177
The study sketch comprises several key elements of the finished rendering: composition, building mass, lighting, entourage, and—interpreted by the viewer—a resultant mood.

Linda L. Mack (1950–1991)
Mentz Residence (IV), page 150
This drawing of the renovation and restoration of the Mentz Residence was published as a poster, announcing a preservation home tour. The challenge was to present a historically significant building from the most utilized viewpoint without losing the three-dimensionality of the building nor its urban setting and without the distraction of adjacent buildings.

"Ornament": Offices for KBJ Architects (IV), page 151
Done in homage to M.C. Escher, this drawing was a corporate Christmas card designed to celebrate the renovation and restoration of a new office and the holiday season. The challenge was to provide a non-denominational image of Christmas which could be used as well for presentation throughout the coming years. The spherical perspective was very challenging, serving to emphasize M.C. Escher's extraordinary graphic skills. Pencil was chosen as a medium to obtain practice in this media.

Philippe Martyniak
Case Western Reserve University (V), page 171
Architects very often request "artistic license" to help in their communication needs. The roof line shown in transparency on the right is a prime example.

Brent A. Maugel, AIA
Chinatown Community Facility (V), page 169
The modernist nature of the structure was enhanced by a
formally balanced composition, a predominantly hard-line
drawing technique, and a high-contrast ink on Mylar
medium. These work in concert with the design to express
the programmatic and cultural purposes of the building.
To set the images in a deep field, and to provide a medium
tone, the sky was painted at varied densities with gray
spray paint. Foreground entourage is restrained to expose
the details of the building and its accurate urban context.

Robert McAllen
Ace Market (IV), page 154
The developer has an unusually artistic stance towards its
projects. This one was already strong enough architectur-
ally to avoid the temptation to do anything "cute." The
illustration was painted in a straightforward manner with
special attention being paid to the glass areas. The mood
was just another sunny day at the beach, which is, after all,
only three blocks away.

James B. McBurney
New Ukrainian Orthodox Church (V), page 193
One of two views, this illustration shows the church on
Easter morning (the other shows Christmas Eve afternoon)
across a marshy, ground-misted area (airbrushed), looking
from the southeast. The sky, windows, and dome under-
painting are transparent watercolor, while the balance of
the paint is opaque watercolor.

Michael McCann
Peaks Competition (III), page 92
Prototypical Atrium Space (III), page 93
University of Southern California at Irvine (IV), page 146

Robert McIlhargey
St. Lawrence Market Complex (III), page 104
This drawing was one of five commissioned to illustrate
proposed architectural changes and the festive character of
a historically important market in Toronto.

Expo '92, Esposicion Universal Sevilla 1992 (IV), page 129
This image, part of two portfolios of 20 illustrations and
master plans, was commissioned to illustrate key site
features and amenities. The views were selected after
careful examination of the project and consultation with
the design team and client group. The objective was to
convey the principal planning concepts as well as the
unique cultural and climatic qualities of Seville, Spain.
The drawings were commissioned for an exhibition to
explain the cultural and planning objectives of the 1992
World's Fair.

Entertainment Complex (V), page 191
Similarly, this aerial perspective was commissioned to
illustrate the conceptual planning and thematic design
principles of the project.

Syd Mead
"L.A. 2015" (II), page 65

Richard C. Meyer
Grace Church (I), page 22
Boathouse, St. Andrew's School (II), page 62
Reconstruction of Hedgerow Theatre (III)
not available for publication.
Adaptive Re-use of Eastern State Penitentiary (III)
not available for publication.

William W. (Buck) Moorhead
Park Avenue Penthouse (IV), page 141
The explosive potential of a brushstroke, the fluidity of oil
paint, and color as defined by the Fauves (wild beasts) are
exploited to capture energy from a Manhattan roofscape.

Martin Myers
Da Vinci Detail (V), page 163
(Category "B" Award, 1990)

William E. Nast
Rock Island Dam (I), page 37
As a member of the architectural design team, the
perspectivist prepared the layout in the office, but the
actual colored pen and ink rendering was completed
at home.

Mark O'Bryan
Monument for the 21st Century (IV), page 147
The project is a towering slab supporting a group of
enigmatic gizmo-like flippers. The moody sky and stark
contrasts of black and white evoke a haunting quality.

Paul Stevenson Oles, FAIA
Canary Wharf (V), page 180
This nighttime detail of the Canary Wharf tower celebrates
the distinctive illuminated pyramidal crown of what is to
be the tallest building in the United Kingdom.

Canary Wharf (V), page 181
The purpose of this nighttime aerial view is to establish
the larger context of the Canary Wharf development
project and indicate its proximity to central London, The
Queen's Greenwich House, and the sinuous Thames.

Orest Associates
Intercontinental Hotel Competition (I), page 29
South Ferry Plaza (V), page 174

Donald Paine
Project for a Gallery (IV), page 141

Marc Partridge
Hemet, California, Urban Masterplan (II), page 48
An attempt to convey the vaporous, abstract notions of
design competitions—their unbuilt nature. This drawing
was composed to describe buildings/potential buildings
while simultaneously related to site location.

Wilbur Pearson
Tequesta Cove (III), page 88
Hinkle Residence (IV), page 126

Benjamin Pilchard
"The Conclusion of an Era...?" (IV), page 124
A tribute to the 20th century, a century of skyscrapers, with a view toward the 21st century, drawn in the familiar style of Hugh Ferriss.

Jeffery S. Poss
Tribute to Olympic Athletes (V), page 186
The Tribute honors county residents who have participated in the Olympics. It marks the first time the official USA Olympic logo has been sanctioned for a community tribute. The simple earthen ramp and concrete archway forms are a metaphor for the process of achievement. The drawing is a developmental study of light and texture, and helped determine logo casting and rustication joint effects in the white concrete.

Antoine Predock
Fine Arts Complex, Arizona State University (III), page 103
Fine Arts Complex, Arizona State University (III), page 103

Eugene V. Radvenis
Hong Kong Expo '97 (IV), page 142
The Expo that never will be—an optimistic celebration of events for Hong Kong in 1997—was an idea promoted by a group of Asian businessmen. The drawing shows the imagined site located on a proposed landfill extending the central financial district into the harbor. The night view suggests the idea of a fair through lighting and simple pavilion forms without a great concern for the architectural reality.

Canada Pavilion, Expo '92 (V), page 184

Dan Raih
20/21 Custom House Street (I), page 39
This massing sketch, executed by a member of the design team, was drawn to convince the Boston Redevelopment Authority that two sensitively designed 12-story buildings would not adversely affect the city's skyline.

Emerson College, Majestic Theatre (II), page 51
One of a series of sketches executed by the architect to stimulate interest in the rehabilitation of an unused and deteriorating landmark building.

Thomas Norman Rajkovich
Chicago Water Works Tower (IV), page 131
A trompe-l'oeil "scroll" (executed in the manner of Piranesi's 18th-century etchings) provides a compositional strategy for the combination of two images in a single drawing. A 0/90 degree axonometry was employed as a means of emphasizing the thematic (iconographic) importance of the new architectural design's formal axial organization, while the existing tower's ruinous state is "revealed" in perspective behind the scroll. As the architectural design itself forms a dialectic between classical and romantic planning principles, the juxtaposition of axonometry and perspective illustration lends contrast and balance.

Yves Rathle
Savannah Aquarium (IV), not available for publication.

Barbara Worth Ratner
Bellsouth Services Headquarters (III), page 104
In response to a sudden request for a drawing indicating preliminary lobby color and material selections, a loose hand with Prismacolor pencils was used to produce a quick and not too literal drawing.

Pier 66 Master Development Plan (IV), page 129
The viewpoint was selected by the architect's client from site photographs, which were invaluable references for the boats. The photos' colors were atypical for Florida, so they had to be imagined. In an experimentation with airbrush work, the clouds, for instance, were done to effect a surreal quality, which works with the postcard colors and simple planes of the building.

The Wave (V), page 189
This piece was created to convey at a glance the playfulness of the forms of this nearly beachfront project.

Michael Reardon
Woodmark Hotel (II), page 69
Waterfront Plan, San Francisco (III), page 102

Capitol Mall Competition (V), page 166
(Juror Award, 1990)

39 Stockton Street (V), page 168
This colorful marketing illustration for a proposed shop in San Francisco accentuates its proximity to the popular shopping district around Union Square, including Macy's and FAO Schwartz. The light typifies San Francisco: the clearing of a storm on a late autumn evening just after work. (This drawing was on the table during the earthquake; the Macy's clock records the time when it struck.)

James Record
The State Capitol Dome (I), page 13
(Best of Show, 1986)

Samuel C. Ringman
S&A Headquarters (IV), page 146
At the entrance to a corporate office facility, the apparent need for a column to support the building is solved by the addition of angels. A Beaux-Arts watercolor approach was used to render this whimsical classical element. The detail was accepted by the client, but the project was not realized since no suitable sculptor could be found.

Cliff House (V), page 196
The romantic nature of this house as it emerges on its dramatic site was enhanced by the low viewpoint and the placement of the stark, geometric forms against the sky. The simple graphic rendering of the architecture and the rough texturing of the rustic setting were achieved through varying combinations of watercolor and pencil.

Richard Rochon

Office Building (II), page 50
The architect very adroitly tucked this office building into a prime but difficult site. The illustration challenge was to depict the building's geometry as well as its relationship to the river and other major office buildings.

Atwater Landing, Detroit (II), page 51
Life on a major waterway takes on a special atmosphere at evening time. Because a series of drawings were done in daylight and at ground level, an elevated view for this overall contextual rendering was chosen.

Peter A. G. Roper

Hydro Quebec Competition (II), page 79
A Polaroid shot of a massing model provided the desired viewpoint for this first crack at a nighttime view.

Addition to Accord Museum (IV), page 138
The clients were firm in their desire to see what the proposed addition would look like in both night and day modes—hence this commission.

City Hall Competition (IV), page 139
The architecture of the competition proposal suggested a curvaceous and dynamic approach to the sketch vignettes; this one took 45 minutes to execute.

Proposed Lighting, Imperial War Museum (V), page 182
A daytime photo of the existing museum served as a guide for architectural details, and the car speeding through a red light is a conjectural illegality.

New Galleria, Grand Central Station (V), page 183
The shadow projection was tricky—a visit to an existing vaulted galleria indicated how the shadows would fall.

Bill Ross

The Alberta Temple (V), page 190
The Alberta Temple in its expansion, refurbishing, and restoration of the Church had architectural features, concealed or lost over time, skillfully restored. Elements of the original building have been shown in the design of the addition, which provides a new formal entrance.

Akira Sato

Adams Residence (I), page 31
The medium, composition, direction of light, and colors for this secluded lake front house were chosen for depicting a mood rather than details of the structure. The entourage is limited to natural landscape elements only in this black-and-white pen drawing. However, color is applied lightly on a printed Mylar, just enough to help to distinguish the elements, water, plant materials, and structure.

Thomas W. Schaller, AIA

"Ideal" English House (I), page 23
"Lutyenesque" forms were assembled to create the illusion of a single structure for this exhibit watercolor. The selection of a partial view was intended to "involve" the viewer—to imagine the remainder of the house without depicting it entirely.

Judiciary Office Building (II), page 62
The requirements for submittals to this competition limited presentations to black-and-white only. The formality and dignity of this neo-classic design work in tandem with existing architecture produce a monochromatic perspective that seems most communicative of its mood and design intent.

125 Summer Street (II), page 63
The sense of drama of late-day sunlight breaking through clouds after a rainstorm and illuminating the tower was the effect chosen to most clearly depict this highly articulated design. Since there is no white pigment in watercolor, the unpainted areas, the white of the paper silhouetted here against a dark surround—gives the work life.

Proposed Arts and Cultural Center (III), page 85
(Hugh Ferriss Memorial Prize Winner, 1988)

Dominus Winery (IV), page 134
One of the artist's chief responsibilities is to accurately portray the relationship between proposed structure and environment. This watercolor demonstrates that a strong, accomplished (though understated) design need not always dominate a beautiful site but rather may work in harmony, or even defer to it.

Proposed Archaeology Museum, Crete (IV), page 135
Architectural fantasies offer the perspectivist an opportunity to experiment with color, color relationships, and architectural forms. This watercolor orchestrated warm and cool tonalities with a range of structural forms in a somewhat unusual and unexpected fashion.

U.S. Courthouse (V), page 188
The contextual nature of this proposal required an interpretive approach to the presentation watercolor. Intricate and important extant foreground buildings had to be accurately portrayed, yet take a visual backseat to the proposed courthouse tower. Areas of sharp focus and contrast were carefully modulated to draw the eye to the subject building. Assisted by Andrew Fitzsimmons.

Federal Triangle Competition (V), page 189
The primary theme of this detailed watercolor was the communication of great physical dimension. Therefore, to enhance the perception of space, modulations of value were utilized in the extreme along with a simplified sense of light to act as visual clues to most clearly delineate fore-, mid-, and backgrounds. Assisted by Andrew Fitzsimmons and Moritosh Nakamura.

Frederic Schwartz, AIA
Quincy Gate (I), page 33

Michael Sechman
First and Mission (II), page 91
Selected entry (V), not available for publication

Robin Sen, RA
CTS Chapel (I), page 28

W. David Shaw
Outdoor Livingroom (II), page 56

Stephen Siegle
Conway Farms South, Chicago (IV), page 125

Rael D. Slutsky and Associates, Inc.
75 State Street (II), page 56
The renderer was asked to highlight the office-tenant uses of the atrium while downplaying the two lower retail levels. The storefront bays are shown with mostly reflective or tinted glazing, with hints of activity within, while the upper office floors are shown with maximum transparency. A separate rendering was later commissioned to focus on retail activity.

75 State Street (II), page 57
The goals of this night-view rendering were to dramatize the building with its lighting scheme and describe materials, colors, and details. The renderer highlighted the setbacks and articulated the massing of the tower on its base. A strong focus was created at the entry arch with the glowing atrium visible behind. The varied colors and surface finishes of the granite cladding are selectively described—giving a sense of the rich detailing without diminishing the impact of the overall image.

One Liberty Place (III), page 94
The strong tower forms, with their faceted tops and spires, are the dominant images portrayed. The reflective glass curtain wall was subdued to avoid "de-materializing" the tower masses, while still lightening the apparent weight of Philadelphia's new tallest building.

One North Franklin Street (III), page 95
A graphic "tryptich" image emerged from the client's desire for an original and powerful portrayal of his design. The vertical format strengthens the focus on the new office building while still depicting the surrounding city fabric. The two outer "panels" of the rendering are toned with a broad "squiggle" stroke of felt-tip pen, but the subject building is better defined with linework and delicate stippling. The black-and-white drawing was Xerox-copied onto a handmade rice paper for coloring.

Bishops Gate, Phase 9/10 (III), page 95
The articulated wood paneling was described in a very detailed manner with pen-and-ink and transparent color pencil media. Natural daylight was used to enliven the mix of materials and surface patterns.

Bishops Gate, Phase 9/10 (IV), page 122
(Juror Award 1989)

100 North Riverside (IV), page 131
The design of this new landmark office building is based on an assembly of "parts" with connecting structural and architectural elements. The rendering viewpoint was chosen to feature the primary vertical building "part"— the clocktower-topped form rising straight up from the plaza. The reflections in the river also support the scale and presence of the tower element.

The Studio of James C. Smith
101 North Wacker Drive (IV), page 156
To best illustrate a redesign and refurbishing of a tower lobby and mezzanine, the drawing features the realignment of the existing corner entrance to the center of the tower. The "parachutist's" view was selected to see the new floor pattern and to create a restrained, surrealistic use of shadows.

Meridian Business Campus (V), page 185
One of a series of three paintings created with minimal use of values, color tones, and depth to portray the architecture in a "stage set" environment. Expression and moods of feeling were very important to create a distinctive character and emit a visual drama.

Richard Sneary
Mid-American Dairymen (IV), page 148
This was one of those rare instances when an image just pops into mind. Never having seen the drawings, a very clear image of the colors and composition developed, much like the final piece, during a phone conversation with the architect. Using a diazo sepia (with a rough, pebbled surface), the print, when drymounted, accepted watercolors in a very unique way, emphasizing its curious texture.

Pickler Library Addition (IV), page 149
The pencil (graphite) and watercolor technique was selected by the architect for its soft, photographic image, finiteness of detail, and the ability to produce both finished black-and-white and color illustrations. The primary issues were the contrast of the old and new parts of the building, the openness and size of the atrium, with its barrel-vaulted skylight, separating the two parts. The view was constructed with a three-point perspective, but controlled to not create severe convergence. By placing the station point at one end of the upper level, the skylight and the visual penetration through and between the bridges to the lower floors were emphasized. A high sun angle, casting light onto the new addition and down to the second floor level, emphasizing the contrast between the older building, in shade, and the new addition, in sunlight.

Hill's Project Quest (V), page 190
The bold use of color and contrasts, responsive to the client's interest in a "painterly approach," place more emphasis on the forms and colors and less on detail.

Henry Sorenson
Big Sky Condominium (I), page 34

R.M. Sovich, AIA
Henderson's Wharf (I), page 21

Thomas A. Spain
Mark and Bonnie Blank Residence (IV), page 136

Gene Streett
River Cottages (I), page 18

Elizabeth H. Sullivan
Residence (III), page 101

Paul Sun, FAIA (1935–1986)
Union College (I), page 28

Tanier Associates
Villa Quadrata (V), page 185
Monochromatic hues present during an early dawn are used to convey the essence of the proposed architectural forms. Absence of color alludes to the serenity to be perpetuated by the future home.

Mongkol Tansantisuk
American Fletcher Building (I), page 17
AT&T Corporate Headquarters (II), page 58
Vanderbilt University (II), page 59
Roseland III (II), page 59

Peter Adrian Thomas
House near Quissett Harbor (I), page 26

Virginia Mahaley Thompson
"Bells, Bells, Bells," (I), page 35
One of five drawings of the original buildings on the Texas Tech University campus featuring the west tower of the Administration Building as framed by the arcade of the old Chemistry Building.

Stefan A. Trendov
Vancouver City Complex (I), page 25
Minnesota Historical Building (II), page 65

James Turner
Broadway Beautification (II), page 55

Stewart White
1629 Connecticut Avenue (IV), page 130
Acrylic airbrush work was used where smooth, even tones and metallic surfaces were needed. The work is predominantly colored pencil on Mylar. The choice of media was selected for the appropriate mood, since each medium has qualities of its own.

Bon-Hui Uy
Plaza view (I), page 27

James Wassell
Cottonwood Trail (IV), not available for publication.

William Wilde (1954-1990)
150 Post Street Renovation (V), page 170

Daniel E. Willis
Edgar Allan Poe Memorial (IV), page 117
(Hugh Ferriss Memorial Prize Winner, 1989)

T. Kelly Wilson
The Pru, Great Galleria (III), page 90
1-2-3 Center Plaza (III), page 91

Shu-Xiang Xi
Maine Medical Center (I), not available for publication.
Old South Church (I), page 21
Kenyon College Library (I), page 42
Smithsonian Institution, Kiosk (II), page 60
73 Tremont Street (IV), page 148

Smithsonian Institution (V), page 197
To depict the most important element of the elevation, a Beaux-Arts ink-brush technique was used and the color applied after the drawing was complete.

Tang Xu
State House Renovation (III), page 86

Tamotsu Yamamoto
Charles River (IV), page 132
One of a drawing series depicting an object sacred to this culture, but in various unexpected arrangements and locations. A very quiet suggestion for people. How people react is not predictable, and it may be understood in different ways. The physical structure—such as rope to support the flag—is not an issue. This drawing was entered partly to spoof the self-seriousness of architectural illustration.

Brad Zeigel
Robbins residence, (IV), not available for publication.